How to Get a New Life

Anna Elsey and Anna Coombes
Edited by Richard Brooks

This book is published to accompany the television series
Get a New Life produced by Brighter Pictures.

Series Editor: Susannah Walker
Executive Producers: Remy Blumenfeld and Gavin Hay

Published by BBC Books, BBC Worldwide Ltd
Woodlands
80 Wood Lane
London W12 0TT

First published 2004

ISBN 0 563 52118 X

Commissioning Editor: Nicky Ross
Project Editor: Sarah Emsley
Copy Editor: Trish Burgess
Art Directors: Sarah Ponder and Annette Peppis
Design: Grade Design Consultants, London
Picture Researchers: Charlotte Lochhead and
Miriam Hyman
Production Controller: Arlene Alexander

Set in Helvetica Neue and OCRB
Printed and bound in France by Imprimerie Pollina s.a. L 93355
Colour separations by Radstock Reproductions.

Anna Coombes was brought up abroad in
South America, Europe and Scandinavia.
Her family moved seven times before she
was ten. She trained as a journalist at a
regional press agency before working
freelance in news and features for the national
newspapers. She has also worked in
television, researching and producing
programmes for Channel 4 and the BBC.
Five years ago she and her husband decided
to escape high house prices and long hours
of commuting in London and relocate to
Scotland where they now live with their
daughter.

Anna Elsey has a long pedigree in both hard
news journalism and feature writing. She
started her career at a major press agency,
covering local stories for regional and national
press and radio. She then helped build a
successful features department for the
agency, writing for all the major weekly
women's magazines. After leaving work to
have a baby, she set up as a freelance writer.
She lives in a Scottish village with her
husband Mark and combines as much writing
as possible with looking after their two small
children, Ged and Florrie.

Contents

Foreword

Get a New Life has tapped into a fantasy that millions of us in the UK seem to share. Many thousands of viewers have written to us asking for our help in relocating to countries as far flung as Australia and New Zealand, and as close to home as Spain, Italy and France. While many of us dream about a new life abroad, very few of us have the courage and commitment to actually make it happen.

So how did it all begin? Two years ago, personal circumstances meant that Gavin Hay and Remy Blumenfeld, the directors of Brighter Pictures, needed to move to San Francisco at short notice. They rented an apartment on-line, hired a car, emailed everyone they knew who'd ever been to San Francisco to see if they had friends in the area, and then made the 12-hour flight to a city they'd only visited twice before.

It was one of the most magical times of their lives. They had a new start in a tiny studio apartment in the shadow of the Golden Gate Bridge and a new life warmed by the California winter sun.

Some months later they returned to the UK and all their friends wanted to know was how they'd done it. Everyone seemed fascinated by the minute detail needed to plan a new life in a foreign country. So, together with the development team at Brighter Pictures, they came up with a TV programme that would make it possible for millions of people to _Get a New Life_ for themselves. As relocators with years of experience between us, we jumped at the chance to be involved with the show.

This book brings together the knowledge and expertise of the whole _Get a New Life_ team so you too can see what it takes to make that move abroad. Firstly, using a series of tasks and questionnaires, we'll help you decide whether you're really ready to up sticks and move your whole life to another country. Then, when you're sure you've made the right decision, we'll show you exactly what you need to do to ensure a smooth and trouble-free departure. Finally, with a country-by-country section packed full of advice and information, we'll help you choose the right location to suit you. It may seem daunting at first but, once you get the ball rolling, you'll see that it is possible to make your dreams come true. There's a new life out there for everyone – you just have to reach out and take it!

Melissa Porter and Scott Huggins

Introduction

Have you had enough of being stuck in endless traffic jams? Cloudy skies and rain, rain, rain? Not wanting to get out of bed in the morning because it's just too cold to bear? Well, you're not alone. At any one time more than half of us in the UK are likely to be at least toying with the idea of moving abroad. And each year some 150,000 people living in Britain make the decision to pack their bags and emigrate permanently.

But simply moving house to somewhere else in the same country is life's third most stressful experience (bereavement and divorce are first and second). Packing up and moving your whole life abroad can go off the stress scale if you don't plan properly. Often it is a long, exhausting, sometimes traumatic process. It's a huge upheaval and one of the toughest choices you are ever going to make. It's not just about better weather, fewer traffic jams and cheaper food. It's about the emotional wrench of leaving family, friends and familiar surroundings. It's about the frustrations of bureaucracy in a foreign language. It's about feeling a million miles away when your mum gets taken into hospital.

To make the right choice, you need to be brutally honest with yourself, your partner and family about why you are doing it and what you expect from life in foreign parts. To make it happen, you need research, planning, patience and a very well-developed sense of humour.

There is no dry run. There is no way of knowing if life will be easier at the other end. But we are here to help you decide if you've got what it takes to follow your dreams and show you how to *Get a New Life*.

1

Making The Right Choice

As you're already reading this book, the idea of living abroad has at least crossed your mind. Maybe you've just got back from a really good holiday, where you've been flabbergasted by how cheap property is, eaten food to die for and drunk wine that cost a tenth of the price it does in the UK. You've been outside in the fresh air, the kids have had loads of exercise, the telly hasn't been on once, and for the entire holiday you kept saying to yourself, 'If only life could always be like this'.

Well, it can – and at the same time it can't. Holidays are holidays and real life is real life. If you find your place in the sun, you'll still have bills to pay, meals to cook and money worries to contend with.

Is It Right For You?

For some, new beginnings are a challenge to be relished, a positive joy. For others, change is frightening, a source of terrible stress. You need to be honest with yourself about the type of person you are.

What are your motivations for moving abroad?
Falling in love with a place on your two-week summer holiday can be a very good reason, or a very bad one, for making a move. In our experience, the single biggest mistake people make is choosing to move abroad on the basis of where they've had a good holiday rather than considering the more fundamental reasons they might be thinking of making a move. On the other hand, if you do your research properly, a great holiday can open your eyes, make you think and eventually lead to a more satisfying and happier life. So don't put a damper on the idea straight away.

Jill and Barry Burgess had wanted to move to southern Spain since falling in love with the area while on holiday in Malaga. Fuelled by their hatred of the British weather, their belief that England isn't a very child-friendly country, and their fear that the UK crime rate was spiralling, they explored the area more fully. After several visits, they set their hearts on Alhaurin el Grande, a small town just outside Malaga. Despite being unsure of what they were going to do for work, the family were certain that the Spanish way of life was right for them and decided to take a huge risk and make the move. Although there have been some stressful periods along the way, the relocation has been a great success and the Burgess family feel that their new life has exceeded all expectations.

We find it helps if you look at the principal areas of your life and ask yourself these two questions:

- What is it about my current life that I'm not satisfied with?
- How will it be better abroad?

Do this now for each of the following topics:

Work
Earning potential
Job satisfaction
Job security
Hours

Working conditions
Holiday entitlement
Time spent commuting

Property
Cost of mortgage or rent
Type of home you live in
Location

Personal
Strength of primary relationship
Family commitments
Children's development

Social life
Contact with friends
Time to pursue hobbies

Now you've answered the questions, you need to get real. Are your expectations about your dream life abroad based on a brief holiday or from what you've seen on TV and in films? If you don't really know how your life will be better, you need to do some serious research and then answer these questions again when you've finished reading this book.

What do I really, really want?
Now you've examined the main areas of your life, we suggest you get totally selfish, and get anyone who'd be moving with you – wife, husband, partner, kids – to do the same. Sit down with pen and paper and give yourselves two minutes to write down your ambitions – as trivial or monumental as they seem. They might include learning a language, writing a novel, going to the opera, taking more exercise, baking bread or just having a set of sexy underwear for every day of the week. It really doesn't matter what you want – just write it down. You'll be amazed by how many thoughts you've got buzzing around in your head. Before you compare notes, look again at your answers and consider what they tell you about the following:

- What is important to you – money, friends, lifestyle, pace of life?
- How do you see yourself in ten years' time?
- How does your vision tie in with the opportunities in the country you are considering?

How Do You Cope With Change?

When answering these questions, write down your answers as soon as they pop into your head, however important or trivial they seem at the time. And don't fool yourself. You need to be brutally honest and not give answers that will convince you to go if, deep down, you don't feel it's the right choice for you.

1. How do you feel about picking up the phone and speaking to someone you've never met?

2. How did you cope with the first day at school/university/a new job?

3. Do you make new friends easily?

4. When you go abroad, do you stick to the tourist scene or go in search of what the locals are up to?

5. Do you thrive on a daily routine?

6. Does the unexpected throw you into a panic or give you a kick?

7. Have you always lived in the same area or have you moved somewhere new before?

8. If you have moved, what effect did it have on you?

9. If you haven't moved to a new area, why not?

10. Could you cope without the security of speaking to your friends or family on a regular basis? (Remember that time differences can make this difficult.)

Now divide your answers into two columns – reasons to stay and reasons to go. How do you feel about moving now? It can be hard to be objective about yourself, so we think it's a good idea to ask a friend to answer some of the questions about you and why you want to leave – with a promise of no recriminations if you don't like what you hear. They could be saving you from a big mistake.

Now compare your wish-list with your family's and you will begin to see whether relocating is really for you. Hold on to your answers and re-evaluate when you've done your research.

Relationships

If you're in a partnership, you must agree that a new life abroad is what you both want, and both have the same agenda. This can't be one person's dream, leaving the other feeling they have no control about what is going on.

If you've taken our advice and got your partner to do the previous exercise as well, then you are at least beginning to get the idea that this is something you are doing together and you both have to feel it is exciting.

Companies who relocate their executives abroad put an awful lot of time into making sure the partner is taken care of, shown around and settled in. That's because they know (and we can testify to this) that the single biggest reason for overseas postings to fail is that the employee's other half has failed to settle.

You must be happy in the couple or family unit you'd be moving with. There will be extra stresses and strains put on relationships by the relocation process and

Strong Enough To Survive?

Here are 20 questions to help you think about the fundamentals of your relationship and if it is strong enough to survive the stresses involved in moving to another country.

1. Do you trust your partner?

2. Are you honest with them?

3. Do you respect their needs?

4. Do they respect your needs?

5. Do you communicate well, talk things through and listen to each other's point of view?

6. Do you work well together and negotiate?

7. What are their five-year, ten-year and lifetime goals? Do they tie in with yours?

8. What interests do you share?

9. What are the qualities you respect in your partner?

10. What do you enjoy doing most with your partner?

11. When did you last get a thrill out of their company?

12. Do you laugh together?

13. When you feel down, does being together make you feel better?

14. Are you financially compatible – in other words, do you have the same attitude to money?

15. Do you show each other affection?

16. Do you both feel appreciated by each other?

17. What are your material goals? You might want to scale down, while your other half might be dreaming of a Mercedes.

18. What do you argue about most – money, sharing housework, lack of respect?

19. Do you feel you each take your fair share of responsibility within the relationship?

20. When deciding what course of action to take, do you discuss it before making a decision?

Now you need to take a hard look at your answers and ask yourself how the problems or assets you have identified might be affected by moving. For example, if you have very different attitudes to money, living with financial insecurity is unlikely to benefit your relationship.

you will have to be strong as a couple or family to survive.

We cannot stress enough that if you think moving will improve your relationship, then you are definitely barking up the wrong tree. Other factors, such as fewer money worries and shorter working hours, may improve the quality of time you have together, but you have to be brutally honest about the strengths and weaknesses of your partnership and face up to the fact that the stresses this move puts on you will only highlight any fundamental problems or weaknesses.

Consider the practicalities. If you both work now, will you both be able to find work when you get there? You both have to be happy and fulfilled.

It is important that your relationship is strong and durable. According to psychotherapist Catherine McMaster, 'You need to know beyond any doubt that you can rely on that other person. The bedfellow of hope is trust. If you can trust each other, you can trust that together you can make it work.'

As well as looking at the fundamentals of your relationship, Relate advises spending time going through the terms on which you are embarking on the move. Consider the following:

- Who wants this move most?
- What are your joint reasons for moving and what are your individual reasons?
- What are you leaving behind and what are you each going to miss most? How are you going to handle this?
- What are your priorities on arrival? One of you might want to explore, while the other might want to get a happy home up and running. How will you deal with different priorities?
- How easily do you make friendships together? Do you like the same type of people?

- How often are you going to make trips back to the UK? One of you might be thinking of three times a year, the other as little as possible. This could impact on how you spend your money.
- What are you going to do about Christmas/ageing parents/important anniversaries?
- What is your biggest fear about the move? Have you shared it?
- Is this for life or have you set a time limit for things to be working out? What is your back-up plan?

Counsellor Paula Hall says, 'You have to go through all the "what ifs" you can think of and thrash them out. If you have thought them through and confronted them, it won't be such a surprise when they occur and you will be better able to deal with them.'

There are no 'right' answers. Every relationship is different, has different dynamics and thrives on a different vibe. Some blossom with excitement and change; others need stability and routine to put down strong roots.

So now is the time to take a good hard look at what it is that makes your relationship tick, and ask yourself if moving abroad is really going to be the best thing for you, and for your relationship.

Remember that you can't solve your problems by running away.

As psychotherapist Catherine McMaster says, 'You don't solve anything by going abroad. If you don't sort out any problems or emotional pain, you'll take it with you as baggage.'

So, however you react to problems here, you'll react in the same way when abroad. You'll still think in the same way and have the same fears and gripes about daily life. What challenges you here will challenge you there.

But Catherine also points out that it is important to remember that you can't solve everything: 'What will become clear is that you can tolerate your problems. Your capacity to cope will grow. So will your self-knowledge. The fact that you have made such a brave move will make you more self-confident. A joy will come from the fact that you have broken a new frontier.'

Relocating your life is a wonderful journey that you've never been on before, during which your confidence will grow and you will learn to trust your intuition and push your self-awareness.

Before *Get a New Life* relocated Philippa Walsh and Pete Docherty to the West Indies, they both thought they had found 'the one' - their partner for life. They'd been together for just under two years and were certain their relationship could take the emotional strain that would be placed on it during the relocation. Sadly, however, following a sometimes rocky relocation where work permits were delayed and dream jobs failed to materialize, just 10 weeks after filming was completed their relationship broke down. But it's not all bad news. Philippa has found a new partner, is still living on Grand Cayman, has an active social life and is thriving. Pete left the island and, as far as we know, is now living happily in America.

Enrolling Friends and Family

To make moving abroad work, you must have the support of your close family and friends, and the earlier you enrol them in the possibilities that you'll be creating for yourself by moving, the better.

Try to be confident. That way your family and friends will also feel confident you'll make it. They must be able to think, 'I can really see them doing this.' That will lead to collective acceptance.

And do your best to transmit your excitement – let them share in it. This is a big thing for them too. Tell them to think of the holidays they'll have when they come to visit. Excitement is infectious. They'll soon be excited too.

It is particularly hard to break the news to an elderly relative, especially a parent who lives alone. It's important to let them know that you've considered their feelings. You have to say, 'I know this will be hard for you and it will leave a hole in your life.' Make it clear, though, that if you don't make the move, you will regret it forever. Let them know it's a great chance to do something you've always wanted, and ask them to be happy for you.

Don't present the decision as a *fait accompli*. It will only deepen the pain if a relative thinks you're doing it regardless of their feelings. Those left behind often feel a sense of abandonment and betrayal. It's a good idea to make an elderly relative feel part of the decision by seeking their approval. Ask for their permission to go. That way they won't feel they are just a bystander watching the process happen around them.

Make it clear that you will miss them, too. Say that you will keep in touch, but in a different way; that instead of seeing them every week, you will write or telephone.

Give them affirmation that your emotional partnership won't stop. Say, 'You'll still be my mum/dad/the kids' grandma or grandad, and we'll still need you.'

When only child Maxine Dilkes packed up her life in Leicester and moved to Brisbane, Australia, with husband Martin and children Norton and Weston, she found that leaving her mother was one of the hardest things she'd ever had to do. Throughout the process of applying for visas, Maxine kept her mum up-to-date with new developments, giving her time to get used to the idea of the move. As you'd expect, there were tears when it finally came to saying goodbye, but Maxine promised to stay in touch regularly, and soon after she arrived in Australia, plans were made for her mum to visit, making her feel part of the whole process.

make a revised checklist of what you want out of your new life. We find it helps to break it down into the specific areas outlined overleaf.

Choosing The Right Country

So you think you've got what it takes to cope with the upheaval of leaving your old life behind and starting a new one abroad? Good for you! It's a brave decision. The next question is, 'Which is the right place for you?'

Perhaps you have already visited your chosen country, fallen in love with it and spent months or years dreaming of starting a new life there. On the other hand, you might not yet know where you want to live. In both cases, you need to apply a little common sense.

If you've followed our advice, you will already have done a lot of thinking. Look back over what you've written down and use it to

It's important to remember that your first impressions of an area may not always be the best indicator, especially if you're on the other side of the world. When *Get a New Life* helped the Dilkes move to Australia, on paper, Redcliffe looked to be an ideal location – clean, close to the sea, with lots of sun, great amenities, a low crime rate and an easy commuting distance to Brisbane. What wasn't immediately apparent, however, was that the majority of the population were retirees, making the area quite unsuitable for a young family. Although further from the sea than they'd originally wanted, the Dilkes finally settled in Carindale, 25 minutes south of Brisbane, which was much better suited to their needs.

What Do You Want?

Ask yourself what you want from each area listed below. Answer the questions in a full sentence, starting, 'I want the possibility of...'

So for 'Job satisfaction', you might write, 'I want the possibility of a job where I look forward to going to work every morning and it doesn't rule my life.' Remember, anything you want is possible if you're determined, but that doesn't have to mean ruthless.

Work
Earning potential compared with cost of living
Job satisfaction
Job security
Hours
Working conditions
Holidays
Language requirements

Property
Cost of mortgage or rent
Type of home
What sort of location you want

Family
Children's education
Standard of healthcare
Social security provision
Keeping in touch with family back home

Social life
Size of expat community
Attitude of locals to expats
Language requirements
What you like doing in your spare time,
        e.g. sports, arts, theatre, etc.

Environment
Sun or snow
Mountains or beaches
Urban or rural

Note: Consider any illnesses that might be affected, for example, asthma tends to be worse in a damp environment.

Using your checklist, now make a short list of countries that appeal to you and find out everything you can about them. Then narrow the list down to regions and ask the following questions:

- Does the population of the area you are interested in reflect your age/interests?
- Is the area vibrant/retirement/up and coming?
- Are there job opportunities to suit one or both of you?
- If you have a particular health problem, are there medical facilities to cope reasonably near by?
- Are your children's educational needs satisfactorily taken care of?
- What is the public transport like? (Worth knowing if you can afford only one car to start with.)
- What is it going to cost to live there and will you be able to afford it?

Effective Research

There are two aspects to making your research as effective as possible. The first and most obvious is finding the information. The second is managing it.

Finding information

The research possibilities for those thinking about relocation are many and various, perhaps even daunting, but there are three obvious places to start.

Internet research can be fantastic. There are sites dedicated to relocating everywhere from Tuscany to Timbuktu. On the down side, it can be time-consuming and you might have to sift through an awful lot of rubbish to get to the information you want.

A good tip when looking for information is to use a search engine from your chosen country. For example, if you want to gen up on New Zealand, use www.google.co.nz rather than its UK counterpart.

Many embassies, consulates and immigration services have comprehensive websites that will answer many of your questions about their countries. The British Consulate in your destination country will also have a website full of local information and numerous links to useful organizations and expat clubs. The Foreign Office is also a good source of facts, figures and statistics.

Check all these sites for links to local newspapers. Some you can subscribe to, others have a selection of stories you can access free of charge. It's an invaluable way of finding out more about the areas you're thinking of moving to.

British and foreign government agencies often have websites with downloadable brochures and forms.

Books are great for in-depth information at your fingertips. A decent guidebook, for example, can provide valuable information about a country, its different regions and any cultural peculiarities. It might even tempt you to look at areas you had not previously considered.

Of course, there are guides to relocating in specific countries, and also many other publications covering specialist subjects, such as buying property abroad and the tax implications of moving overseas.

Telephone research will help you to find what you can't locate on screen or in print. Probably the quickest way to track down someone who can help is to consult the embassies and consulates section in the *Yellow Pages*.

The consulate of the country you are considering is always a good starting point for further information. If you can't get through (they're always very busy), you could talk to a removal company or relocation specialist who deals with the country. You could also try telephoning the relevant government department. For example, if you want to find out about exporting your car, phone the DVLA; if you want to know about health cover abroad, try the Ministry of Health.

It is also worth asking your bank to send you any information they have on financial issues arising from your move, such as buying property, making a will and paying tax. They might even have a sister company in the country you're going to, which can make life much easier.

Managing your research

You will very quickly amass a great deal of information, and you must find a way of keeping it accessible and understandable.

Everyone has a preferred way of working. Some people like doing everything on their computer, others prefer reading things on paper. Both methods require systematic organization.

Make sure you have a notepad dedicated to researching the move so that, for example, Spanish tax details don't get thrown out with last week's shopping list.

Now make yourself a filing system. We suggest you create files (computer or cardboard) under the following headings, which reflect those used in this book.

- Visa/residency requirements
- Pets
- Household goods/Removal firms
- Car/Driving licence
- Property
- Job opportunities
- Health
- Money matters
- Education
- Leisure

Use it or lose it

You will come across a huge amount of information – far too much to keep – so discipline yourself to file only what is useful. It will save time and energy and stop you getting frustrated when you can't find something.

Internet research is both marvellous and maddening in its scope. To ensure you can retrace your steps if you have to, save web pages to a 'Favourites' file, or print them out as you go along. This will prevent you doing the same work twice and save time when you want to revisit sites (you can't rely on search engines throwing up the same results every time). In addition, if the site suffers problems just when you need access, you'll be very glad you kept hard copies.

Identify what is useful. If a whole page or article is helpful, print it out and file it. If there are just one or two useful facts on a page, make a note of them and where you found the information, then file it. Chuck out irrelevant stuff: sifting through it time and again is frustrating and pointless.

Books are wonderfully accessible. Being indexed makes them quicker to flick through than any website, and you can use them just about anywhere. Use a highlighter pen or Post-it™ notes to mark useful information, then transfer it to the appropriate section of your research files.

Telephone research requires careful note-taking, so always make sure you have pen and paper to hand. Start with a clean page for each call and write the number, the organization and, where you know it, the name of the person you want to speak to. Of course, always be polite; it really can help you to get the assistance you need.

Make notes of the information you are given as you go along – don't rely on remembering everything afterwards – and always ask if there is any relevant information they can send you. If your informant has been especially helpful, ask for their direct line and email address so that you can contact them again and build up a relationship.

When you put the phone down, go over your notes and flesh them out so they are clear when you come to look at them later. Finally, put them in your relevant file.

The best defence against failure is knowledge coupled with common sense. Do your homework, use your head and only engage your heart when it comes to the final decision.

Visiting The Country

However much research you do, there is nothing quite like being in a place to get the real picture. What you're undertaking is momentous and life-changing, so it's worth taking the time to ensure the dream does not turn into a disaster.

Where possible, and if your annual holiday allows, it's best to make a series of extended stays, about a month or so each, at different times of the year. Of course, if short stays are all you can manage, they're definitely better than nothing.

These stays should not be regarded as holidays, but as exercises in familiarization.

Regular visits like this will help you get to know the local community. Make use of them: they will have invaluable advice on everything from doctors to dog walkers, so, before you go, make a list of what you want to achieve and the information you want to bring back. This can make the whole experience a lot more relaxing.

Never turn down an invitation to visit a local's home. Ask them why they bought the type of home they did, what mistakes they made, how they might do things differently. Used wisely, this local knowledge might also open up job opportunities or lead to you hearing about a house for sale before it goes on the market.

Investing time and money in exploratory trips is rarely a waste. You will be making a choice based on real knowledge of the place you want to go to, and could arrive with a job, house and social circle all in place. That is a relocator's dream situation.

2

Making It Happen

Having read Chapter One and answered key questions, you should now have established whether relocating is right for you. You might also have some idea as to which country you want to emigrate to and the practicalities involved in moving there. Now you need to make it happen.

If a non-English-speaking country is top of your list, we cannot overstress the importance of speaking the language. Without fluency you will severely limit your job opportunities, and technical vocabulary may be essential for certain occupations. For example, a doctor relocating to Spain will need to be able to write prescriptions in Spanish. Even if you're, say, an aromatherapist in Italy with only expat clients on your books, you'll still need specialist vocabulary to order supplies. So ask yourself if you speak the language:

- Not at all
- Enough to order a beer
- Enough to have a chatty conversation
- Well enough to understand a legal contract, discuss drains with a plumber, attend a school parents' evening and argue about politics.

Unless you give the last answer, it is going to be in your interests to enrol for classes straight away. All too often, learning the language is left until the last minute, or even until arrival, but the more work you put into it now, the better, and the easier it will be to settle in and become part of the community. It will probably be at least several months, if not a year, before you are ready to leave the UK, so start now and you could have advanced your skills considerably by the time you leave.

Set the ball rolling and contact your local college or university to find out more about available courses. The sooner you start, the better your language skills will be when you arrive, the easier things will be for you, and the better your chances of success.

Planning Your Departure

The length of time it takes to organize your move will vary greatly according to where you are going and what your circumstances are. You should allow at least three months for organizing the practicalities of moving, but remember to take into account three other important factors:

- How long will the bureaucracy take?
- When will you be in a strong financial position to make the move?
- What other factors will affect when you go, e.g. schooling?

Bureaucracy

Each country has its own vastly different immigration requirements. The first port of call should always be the consulate, embassy or high commission of the country of your choice. They can provide a wealth of information on entry requirements and general relocation issues. If you're moving within the EU, the process of relocation is relatively straightforward. You do not need a visa, so in theory you can pack up and go whenever you like.

Anywhere outside the EU is a whole different ball game. Emigrating to Australia, for example, can take anything up to two years; New Zealand, one month to a year; so speak to the relevant consulate and plan your timescale according to what you're told.

If you are moving outside the EU, there is no guarantee that your application will be successful, so do not make any arrangements

for moving until things are set in stone. In one case we know of a family emigrating to Canada, the father had his application rejected at the eleventh hour because the authorities decided the job he had got could be done by a Canadian. The family got there in the end, but it was touch and go, and extremely stressful, as they had already given notice on their rented house, sold most of their possessions and spent £4,000 on removals and transporting their two dogs to Canada.

Always do things in this order:
- Gather information for your application
- Prepare and submit your application
- Wait for the result
- When successful, *only then* should you make practical arrangements.

Application procedures can be complicated, so if the process really does seem too daunting, it could be worth hiring the services of a specialist visa and immigration consultant (see pages 156–157). These experts might seem expensive at first, but could save you time and stress, and ultimately make the difference between a successful or an unsuccessful visa application. They can also help you with settling in at the other end, help you find an area you like, a home and schools for the children.

When moving to Lucca, Itlay, in series one, Elidh Smith and Mike Austin-Eames found dealing with Italian bureaucracy to be extremely difficult, especially as different government departments had different opinions as to whether Elidh's chiropody qualifications were valid or not. Being unable to speak the language only added to their frustration as they had to rely on other people to translate for them.

Money

Take a cold, hard look at your financial situation. You need to plan ahead and answer some searching questions before making a move.

What are your debts?

Try to pay off your debts before you go: there are many practical options for doing so. The biggest asset you have is probably your home. Selling your house and renting something smaller until you leave might seem drastic, but if you're definitely emigrating, it's an option worth taking. If you have two cars, consider selling one. You could also sell furniture that you don't intend taking with you. You'll be surprised what you can give up for a brief period of time to achieve your long-term goal.

If you have multiple loans, concentrate on paying off the most expensive first, and, if you can, increase your monthly repayments. Even a few extra pounds can make a considerable difference to the interest you pay. If tackling your debt seems too daunting, seek help from an independent financial adviser.

What does it cost you to live?

Keep records of all your outgoings so that you have a realistic idea of what you spend your money on. Research the cost of living and average wages for your profession in your chosen country. What wage will you realistically need to survive?

Do you have any savings?

You will need a nest egg to fall back on when the going gets tough. What assets could you sell that you won't need abroad? Do you have business assets, such as premises, a website or a client base, that you could dispose of?

What will it cost you to make the move?

Think about the costs involved in selling your present home, such as the solicitor's and estate agent's fees. Think about the costs of buying your new home, such as the equivalent of stamp duty, and legal fees. Then think about other costs, such as removal and shipping fees, travel and everyday expenses (food, clothes, utilities, etc.) until you are established. Will you stay in a hotel while you find somewhere to live? How much will it cost?

How are you going to make your living?

How employable are you? Do your skills match those needed in the area you're going to? What salary do you need to live? If you want to set up a business abroad, is it competitive? Are there other similar businesses in your chosen area? Are your qualifications recognized? What will it cost you to set up?

We really can't stress enough the importance of having a plan of action for when you arrive. In our experience, people who say they'll do anything when it comes to finding employment in a foreign country usually don't make enough money to maintain their standard of living, which can be a major factor in relocations failing. You have to be realistic about what you need to live on and what you are willing to do without.

Other factors

Among the things that might impinge on when you make a move are the dates that children start school; the low season, when temporary accommodation is cheap; the high season, when there might be more work opportunities.

Getting Ready To Go

Once you have addressed all the issues outlined above, you can begin to prepare for your move. By drawing up a plan of attack along the lines suggested below, you can do much to mitigate the inevitable stress levels.

1. Selling up and clearing the clutter

If you are a home-owner your biggest decision is likely to be what you are going to do with your property. Will you sell it for a large cash injection or rent it out for regular income?

Bear in mind that if you rent out your home, you'll probably have to pay an agent to manage the let. Also, you will have to allow for the property lying empty between lets.

Whatever you decide, make your house as marketable as possible. Make sure you do all those little jobs that could put off buyers or tenants. You'll need every penny when you get to the other end, but don't rule out giving your house a fresh lick of paint. A clean, bright, well-kept house really can influence how potential buyers think about the property and the price, and the speed with which your home is sold.

Use the move as an opportunity for a really good clear-out. A tidy, ordered home will be more desirable. It will also get you to assess what you really need to take with you. Boxes in the attic that haven't been opened since your last move can probably be chucked. You can obviously live quite happily without whatever is in them. Psychologically, it is a good thing to do, and financially, it will mean you do not pay any more for your removal than necessary and that you get the best rent or sale price possible.

We love Dawna Walter's *Life Laundry* advice to keep only what you use or what you love – the rest can go.

You will need
- Strong boxes
- Newspaper for wrapping breakables
- Labels to identify contents and where they are to go
- Rubbish bags.

Discard
- Anything that has been broken for 12 months or more
- Anything past its use-by date
- Old technology
- Electronic or electrical goods not compatible with your destination
- Books you no longer use
- Items associated with hobbies you no longer pursue
- Unnecessary papers, magazines, junk-mail, files and paperwork
- Outgrown toys and kids' clothing
- Furniture that is broken or that you don't use
- Boxes unopened since your last move
- Clothes that no longer fit, suit your lifestyle or haven't been worn for 12 months.

Sell, recycle or dump?
- Investigate the local car boot sale.
- Contact local antique dealers to assess valuable items.
- Advertise unwanted items in good condition in the local newspaper or in the newsagent's window.
- Have a sale at home: invite your friends round, or advertise it as a garage sale.
- Find out from charity shops what they will accept.
- Paper, glass, cans and plastics can be recycled.
- Get advice from your local council about disposing of anything combustible or poisonous.

2. Move yourself or be moved?

If you're relocating within Europe, transporting your possessions isn't generally too costly or difficult. Many people choose to rent a van and do the move themselves. Just make sure you have an inventory in case customs do decide to stop you. Also make sure you have contacted the relevant customs authority to check for any banned items. Firearms, plants and certain breeds of dog could all be subject to an import ban.

For moves outside Europe, most people use a removal firm, but there's nothing to stop you liaising direct with a shipping company. You could even arrange for your goods to go out in the empty refrigeration units of returning ships, which can cut costs. However, reputable removal firms do have the added benefit of customs and procedural knowledge, which can smooth the move considerably.

Bear in mind that removal companies generally calculate the cost of moving items according to volume, not weight. So if you've got a box of cherished photos or magazines, it would be worth taking them with you, but that moth-eaten old sofa is best left behind. Buy a new one when you get there.

You might also want to consider taking a small package of your family's possessions by air freight. Obviously there's no hard and fast rule, but have copies of all your documentation to hand, including any permits, insurance, bank statements, references and police checks if you had any carried out in the UK. A first-aid kit, a basic tool kit, bed linen, clothes, children's toys, maps, and a few sentimental items can all make moving into a new place while most of your belongings are packed up a whole lot easier. It might be expensive, but it could make life so much more pleasant when you get there.

If you are flying to your destination, it is worth telling the airline when you book your seats that you are emigrating. You might get a better baggage allowance.

Choosing a Removal Firm

- Obtain at least three quotes from reputable companies, preferably ones recommended by family and friends. Don't just consider cost. Does the company seem helpful and efficient? Trust your gut instinct – it counts for a lot.
- Make sure the company uses its own staff, not subcontracted labour.
- Ask to see references for moves similar to yours.
- Check the limits insurance companies offer. Arrange additional insurance if necessary.
- Big removal companies, such as Crown or Pickfords, have brochures with useful hints for movers.

Countdown

Moving is stressful, no matter what the distance involved. But with careful planning the stresses can be minimized. By drawing up an agenda for dealing with the practicalities, you can leave yourself time for dealing with the emotional upheaval of this life-changing event. This will help you to arrive at the other end better organized, less stressed and more able to make the most of your new life from day one.

Adjacent is a guide to what needs doing when. Of course, you can tailor it to your requirements and do it more quickly or more slowly. The pace is in your hands.

Three months before you go

- Start making a complete inventory of things you are taking. Keep it somewhere safe and add to it as necessary. If you have receipts, keep them with your inventory. For goods without receipts, put an estimated price for each item.
- Start using up frozen food and those tins and packets in the back of cupboards.
- Inform your children's schools that they will be leaving and ask for their school records.
- Check importation requirements for your car, or get it ready to sell.
- Check importation requirements for your pet. (If possible, this should be done six months before you leave, as some countries require a rabies vaccination to have been done six months before the animal enters the country.)
- Start keeping a record of moving expenses with receipts. If your employer has agreed to pay your relocation costs, you may be able to claim some or all of them back. Also, check with your local tax office whether any costs are tax deductible.
- Arrange storage facilities and check both your own and the storage company's insurance policies give you adequate cover.
- Find a removal firm and check their insurance cover.
- Arrange flights, hire car and accommodation for your arrival – particularly if you are arriving in high season.

Two months before you go

- Contact your bank and tell them of your move. Find out what services they offer to relocators. Remember to keep a UK bank account so that you can arrange for a direct debit into your overseas bank account (once you have one) until you are completely established in your new home.

- Inform your doctor you are leaving and ask for your medical records. Also inform your dentist, optician and any other health practitioners that you will be leaving.
- Begin packing items you don't use very often. Remember to add each item to your inventory.
- Begin collecting your important documents in a fire-safe box. You will need the following originals:
  - Educational qualification certificates
  - Birth certificates for all your family
  - Your marriage certificate
  - Medical records, including children's inoculations – you may need these to register them for school
  - Professional qualification certificates
  - Work references
  - Passports
  - Children's school reports
  - Wills
  - Pet documents.
- Get multiple photocopies of all your documents and leave a complete set with a friend, relative or solicitor. Make sure someone close to you knows where they are.
- Arrange for a translation of any documents stipulated by the embassy or consulate.

A month before you go

- Notify the following services that you are leaving the country, or cancel them:
  - Utilities (gas, electricity and telephone)
  - Post Office (find out about setting up a forwarding service. The most reliable method is to get a Post Office re-direction

to a friend or relative, and ask them to forward the important items to you)
  - Council tax office
  - Insurance companies (arrange insurance to cover the move)
  - Clubs (if membership cannot be refunded, ask about transferring it to a friend)
  - Newsagent
  - Subscriptions
  - Milkman
  - Any voluntary organizations you belong to.
- Clear out lockers and desks at work and school. Use just the bare minimum until the move. Remember, anything you want to take with you needs to be packed, ready for shipping.
- Arrange to transfer valuables, such as jewellery, cash and essential documents. Do not send valuables with your moving company. Either carry them with you – invest in a lockable box – or send by insured registered mail.
- Arrange for safe disposal of combustible

and environmentally unstable items, such as paint cleaners, oil-based paints and lighting fluids. Ask your local council for details.

- Get a floor plan of your new home and decide which furniture is going where. Use different coloured stickers for each room, and give the removal men a copy of the code. It will make things easier at the other end.
- Send out invitations for your leaving party, if you are having one.

Two weeks before you go

- Return or reclaim all items you have borrowed or lent.
- Return library books.
- Collect all outstanding dry cleaning, shoe repairs, etc.
- Clean curtains and rugs and do laundry so that things arrive clean.
- Prepare meals in advance for these last two weeks so that you can keep shopping to a minimum.

A week before you go

- Store clean bed linen and pillows in chests of drawers if you are taking furniture with you. That way you'll be able to lay your hands on what you need to spend your first night in your new home in comfort.
- Prepare your emergency pack of essentials to carry with you. Include:
  - Clothes suitable for when you arrive
  - Toys to keep the kids happy
  - All your essential documents
  - A torch
  - Prescription medicines (ask your doctor for the generic name, as brands vary between countries)
  - An extra pair of glasses or contact lenses

- A travel alarm
- First-aid supplies

The day before the move

- Finish packing anything you are taking with you.
- Gather together all house, garage and shed keys. Arrange to leave them with the new owners of your home, your solicitor, your estate agent, your letting agent, or a trusted neighbour.
- Give a close friend or family member a list of your itinerary in case of an emergency. You could arrange to telephone at a few pre-arranged times until you are safely at your destination.

The day of the move

- Check your removal firm's inventory to make sure you agree with it. Get a copy of their inventory.
- Search every room to make sure you've left nothing behind.
- Give the house a final clean.
- Leave a forwarding address.
- Check that all windows and doors are locked.
- Remember tickets, money and passports.

Arrival

- Check that all the utilities are working.
- Let family and friends know you have arrived safely and inform them of new telephone number.
- Unpack the necessary basics.
- The kitchen and the children's rooms should be your first priority.
- Give the kids a job to do. Starting to sort out their rooms will make them feel at home straight away.

Moving Emotions

Moving is not all about practicalities – you need to take care of your personal wellbeing too.

The countdown to departure is a transitional period – your heart won't be in your old life, but you haven't yet started your new one. Stay positive. Remember why you're doing this. The reason is a happy one – to make your life even better, to fulfil a dream. Try to feel excited, not permanently stressed.

Of course, there will be stress to contend with – from the hassle of sorting out a removal firm to the heartache of disposing of familiar possessions. Things won't always go according to plan and there'll be upsets along the way. Then there's the stress of leaving behind support structures – not just family and friends, but familiar surroundings that make you feel grounded.

You're going on an emotional journey, not just a physical one. You have to face the possibility that it might not work out. But if it doesn't work, you can come back. Chances are, you'll be coming back because you want to, not because you have to.

Children

Stay positive in front of your kids, even at those times when you wonder what on earth you're doing. Talk to them – tell them what's happening, why you're moving, where you're going to. Let them help so that they feel involved.

Listen. Ask them how they're feeling. Leaving friends, family and familiar surroundings is scary. If their feelings are negative, empathize and reassure them.

Try to time your relocation so that children can start school soon after arrival. It would be hard for them to be in a new place with little chance of making friends for a long time.

Before you go, at least get prospectuses for all the schools in your area. If you are able try to arrange their places before you go, it will lessen their sense of uncertainty. Remember that children will react differently to the move, depending on their ages.

Pre-school children can be rather unsettled by the move. Mum and Dad are constantly busy and all their favourite things are being packed away. The most important thing is to make them feel secure and involved, so don't always pack little ones off to a babysitter – let them stay with you sometimes and help.

Primary school children are bound to feel a bit anxious, so make the experience exciting. Tell them about the new friends they'll make, the new places they'll see. Tell them as much as possible about what is going to happen. The more they know, the more confident they will feel.

Teenagers will probably be the most unsettled by the move. Friends are especially important to them, and moving away will be hard. Buy them an address book to write down their friends' contact details. Reassure them that the new friends they make will be welcome in your home. Tell them you will help them to join the local football team, swimming club, art class – whatever they're interested in. Suggest they research the area they'll be going to so that they feel involved and get excited.

Coping With Loneliness

Don't let the fact that you're missing loved ones become a negative influence on your life. Here are our top tips:

- Store up your wonderful experiences and recount each one in your next letter or phone call.
- Set a date for when you will see the folks back home and think how wonderful it will be, even if that time is a long way off. Think of everything you'll have to show them when they visit you.
- Think how lucky you are. You'll never fall into the trap of taking your loved ones for granted. Every time you see them will be special. You may not see your loved ones as often as you'd like, but you've swapped quantity for quality.
- Unpack photos and mementos to remind you of home and bring a smile to your face.
- Send photos or children's drawings back home to keep friends and family feeling involved in your life. Ask them to do the same for you. This is particularly important if you have children.

Getting Established

Once you've jumped the highest hurdle and are actually living in your dream location, it's time to look at how to go about settling in. We've found that making friends and feeling at home are things we take for granted in our home country as they're part of an ongoing process in a familiar environment. But when you're starting from scratch in a completely new country you might find you need to relearn some of the essential skills that will help you on your way. This might feel a little intimidating, but remember that it's part and parcel of getting the new life you've been dreaming of.

Mixed emotions

Settling in is a time of great excitement and expectation tempered with disappointment and frustration. One minute you'll be on the top of the world, dizzy with all you've achieved, all the new sights and sounds around you, and the wonderful experiences you know are to come. The next you'll wonder what on earth you've done and why you left behind all that was safe, comfortable and familiar.

Be prepared for all these feelings and more. We've found that everybody, to some extent, goes through a whole gamut of emotions no matter how much they've tried to prepare for moving. The best way of coping is to embrace what you're feeling as an important part of the whole experience, and learn to put your emotions in context. The newness is part of the move and helps make it special.

When you feel down, remind yourself why you made the move. Try to make time for a trip to the beach, a walk in the countryside or a slap-up meal in a local restaurant. It will remind you what it was that attracted you to your new life.

Give yourself a pat on the back. You've

done well to get this far. Most people are still only dreaming about doing what you've done. After all you've achieved so far, the coming year will present little that you can't deal with.

This will be a busy time and there will be periods of hard work, so it's important to remember to devote time to your family and to your own wellbeing. Make sure you set aside time for a family treat, and spare some time for yourself, as it's all too easy for life to become a long list of things to do. Believe us, there will be times when you'll wonder if you weren't better off in the UK, but these moments will pass.

Be aware of how the rest of the family is feeling and what they might be finding difficult; don't block them out. Saying, 'Well, there's nothing I can do about that. We're here now,' will only make them feel disempowered and even more homesick. Be sympathetic and listen to their feelings.

Make offers of help. If a teenager is worried about making friends, say you'll help them enrol at a local youth club, and ferry them back and forth every week. Or let them invite a couple of schoolmates for a sleepover.

We've found it's a good idea to get the whole family to commit to eating dinner together in the evening. After all, one of the prime reasons that many families want to relocate is to spend more time together. So turn off the television and talk; this is a time when talking will really benefit everyone.

Don't forget your partner. If you're working and your other half isn't, they could be feeling isolated. Offer reassurance, tell them how much you love them and how you enjoy spending time with them. Arrange a night out with work colleagues and their spouses so that they don't feel left out. Even better, make time where the two of you can be alone or go on a date.

Remember that there will be times when

things don't go according to plan. Accept that there will be hiccups along the way. Perhaps the water won't be on when you get to your new home. Or maybe buying the house of your dreams falls through at the last minute. There's no limit to the number of things that can go wrong, no matter how thoroughly you plan. When one of the families we relocated to New Zealand finally sold their house in the UK, they thought transferring money and buying their new house would be simple. What they hadn't counted on was an internal delay at their UK bank, which held up the transfer and lost them over £1,000 as the exchange rate dropped.

Of course, things can go amiss anywhere. The flipside is that you'll get some nice surprises along the way, and sometimes things will prove easier than you thought. And we guarantee that somewhere along the line you'll be on the receiving end of help or generosity you didn't expect.

On a practical note, have some cold remedies on stand-by. The stress of moving can weaken your immune system, and 'movers' flu' is well known in the expat world.

Take your time

Feeling at home in a new country doesn't happen in a few days. It could take weeks, months or even years. You're bound to feel unsettled and homesick for a while, but don't give up too quickly. Be realistic. We know one lady in her seventies who emigrated to Australia as a £10 Pom over fifty years ago. There are still things she misses about the UK, even though she has a fantastic life Down Under. On balance, she wouldn't change a thing.

You must give your new life a fighting chance, and we think that means a year at the very least. Set a realistic timescale. Say to yourself, 'I won't even think about going home until I've given it a year/eighteen months/two years' – whatever you've decided.

If that seems too long, we've found it helps to break the time down and set yourself targets. You might decide, for example, that in three months you want to have started an evening class, found a good nursery and explored the region you've moved to more fully to decide exactly where you want to live. By setting yourself realistic, short-term targets, you'll be able to recognize your achievements and start to feel more secure.

Tell yourself, 'I'll see how I feel in three months' time.' Then give yourself another three months, and another… Before you know it, you'll be feeling like part of the furniture.

Missing friends and family

Settling in will be the loneliest aspect of moving. You'll miss loved ones, but won't yet have made new friends. Remember, this is a temporary state of affairs and it will get better.

You have to accept that there will be times when you feel isolated and lonely, and miss special people in your life. If you've had a bad day, you won't be able to just pop round to your mum's and tell her how you feel. Even ringing your best friend for a chat might be tricky if you've moved far away and the time difference means that one of you is sleeping while the other is working.

The most important thing to remember is that, emotionally, you need to be gentle with yourself. You're suffering a huge loss, so expect to feel sad. You must accept that this is a sacrifice you had to make; it's the cost of your wonderful new life.

Meeting people

Many new relocatees are bowled over by the warmth of the welcome they receive. Most people embrace new members of their community with open arms. Chances are you'll have invitations for coffee before you've finished unpacking. And remember, people who make friendly gestures are not just being kind; even those who have lived somewhere for ages are glad of the opportunity to make new friends.

Making friends

- Go and introduce yourself to your new neighbours as soon as possible. Taking a little gift is a nice touch – perhaps a cake, or flowers or fruit from your garden.
- Ask your neighbours round to your house for coffee or a glass of wine if they haven't asked you first. *Voilà* – instant friends!
- Chat to your postman, local shopkeeper, electrician – anyone you come across in the course of your everyday life. Tell them you're new and ask their advice about what is going on in the area – events coming up, good restaurants, friendly bars. Remember that no matter where you move to, most people love the opportunity to help and give advice. Not only will you glean useful snippets of insider knowledge, but chances are someone will invite you out with them, or ask you round to their home.
- If you live in a small community, check out the hub of local life. If it's a village shop, for example, chat to the shopkeeper. That way, word about you will spread, and people will be on the lookout for you, wanting to find out more.
- If you have children, you'll hit the ground running because kids are an endless source of new friendships. Get chatting to other parents at the school gate. Introduce yourself, ask their children's names, what class they are in. You have an instant common interest. Get involved with the running of the school – committees, fundraising events, after-school sports meetings. If your kids

are invited to a new friend's home after school, go and pick them up – and make sure you meet the parents.

- If your children aren't at school yet, there are still ways to meet other mums and dads. Most places have a toddler group run by parents, where you can drop in for coffee and a chat. Ask around, or look in the local press to find your nearest. Or, if your kids are no longer toddling, get involved with the local playgroup. Giving up a little of your time to attend committee meetings or look after stalls at fundraisers can reap enormous rewards in terms of making friends.

- Don't neglect your hobbies. If you enjoy golf, join your local club. If you're a keen sketcher, sign up for an art evening class. If you're good at football, train with your local five-a-side team. Join a flower-arranging class, a bungee-jumping club, your local am-dram group – anything. It might be a cliché but we don't care – what could be better than friends who love what you love?

- If you are working, you have an instant circle of potential pals.

- Contact your nearest British Consulate to find out about expat organizations in your area.

- Enrol at a language class. Although your proficiency in a foreign tongue will come on in leaps and bounds because you're using it every day, it is still a good idea to have proper long-term tuition. And you'll make friends to boot, no doubt including other Brits.

Mind your manners

- Don't be too pushy. There's nothing more off-putting than someone trying to muscle in on your life and wanting

to be your best friend straight away. Psychotherapist Catherine McMaster says, 'Avoid the gush and slush approach. Take things steady. Making real friends doesn't happen overnight. Just relax and enjoy the experience of getting to know someone.'

- Familiarize yourself with the social customs of your adopted home. That way you'll make sure you don't drop an embarrassing clanger.

- Always be polite. It is better to be over-formal when addressing people you don't know too well than to be too familiar and risk offending them. Await permission to be more familiar, especially with people older than you.

- Let people know you are committed to getting involved in the life of the community and that you're not just passing through. Outside big cities, locals understandably object to people buying holiday homes and pushing up prices but not contributing to the community.

- Be open. Tell people about yourself and your family. Knowing who you are and what you're about helps people warm to you. That way they'll be open and friendly with you too.

So you've done it – you've got your new life. The only thing that remains is for us to say 'Good luck and go for it!' We'd love to hear how you get on.

3

European Union

Ah, the EU. Grey men in grey suits making reams and reams of boring, pointless bureaucracy. Right? Wrong. The EU is your friend. Anywhere else in the world, relocation is a mind-bogglingly complicated business. But if you are moving within the EU, take heart: as a citizen of a member country, you have rights that will help to soothe many relocation headaches.

The good news is that, subject to certain conditions, any EU national is entitled to move freely in other EU countries, to work, study or retire, and enjoy the same rights as nationals of that country. So, although there is still red tape to unravel, the EU really is your oyster.

EU member states

The countries that make up the EU are interestingly diverse – some industrial and prosperous, others less developed and less wealthy. The current members are: Austria, Belgium, Denmark, Finland, France, Germany, Greece, Ireland, Italy, Luxembourg, The Netherlands, Portugal, Spain, Sweden and the UK.

On 1 May 2004, ten new EU member states will be created: Cyprus, the Czech Republic, Estonia, Hungary, Latvia, Lithuania, Malta, Poland, Slovakia and Slovenia.

Allied to the EU as European Economic Areas are Iceland, Norway and Liechtenstein. Although not actually members of the EU, these countries are subject to most of the rules relating to other EU nations.

Get There

Hurray! You don't need a visa to move to another EU country. There is no lengthy application process, no points system, no long list of entry requirements. Theoretically, there is nothing to stop you chucking your things in a van and leaving tomorrow. Obviously, however, things get a little more complicated when you arrive, so it pays to do your homework before you go.

In these days of budget air fares, many places in Europe are cheap and easy to get to. We recommend that you always, always visit a place at least two or three times before you seriously consider moving there – and not just for two weeks of sizzling on a beach either. Try to stay longer, have a really good nose around and try it in different seasons: that idyllic little spot you found in the middle of summer might be insufferable in the depths of winter.

If you're worried about making the commitment, don't fret – you can stay for up to three months in another EU country with no need for paperwork or permits. All you need is a valid identity card or passport.

In some countries you may be asked to inform the authorities of your presence, though in most cases, this happens automatically, such as when you check into a hotel.

Right of Residence

As an EU national, you are entitled to a residence permit for a stay over three months in any other EU state, subject to conditions based on your circumstances.

How do I get my residence permit?
The good news, if you are on a tight budget, is that there's little or no cost involved. Your permit has to be issued either free of charge, or for the same fee a national pays for an identity card.

When you get to your chosen country, go to the relevant issuing authority. This is usually the local police station or town hall, but it does differ from country to country. The European Commission's Europe Direct website (see page 154) will tell you where to go in each country for your permit. Sounds simple? Well, things are never as easy as they first appear.

Getting your hands on a residence permit will involve lots of waiting around, wading through forms and running between offices. Then there are all the officials shaking their heads and gesticulating, apparently put on this Earth with the sole purpose of making your life as difficult as possible. All you can do is grin and bear it. But just remember – once it's over, you won't have to go through the agony again and you'll have completed the crucial first step to your new life.

Your permit is valid for five years and is automatically renewable. Students, however, are not so lucky, as their permits have to be renewed annually. All permits are also valid in a country's dominions, and remain valid even if you go away for up to six months. Whatever your status, when applying for a residence permit, you will always need to show a valid passport or identity card. You may also be asked for other documentation (see pages 35–6).

How right of residence affects you
Your right to stay in an EU country is dependent on what you do while you are there. The following situations cover most eventualities.

If you are working
If you want to go abroad for between three months and a year for a temporary job or self-employed work, you are entitled to a residence permit for the period you are there. You will also be issued with a permanent residence permit to live in another EU country for good if you have a job or are self-employed. You are entitled to work before your residence permit is issued.

In theory, you do not need a work permit to work in an EU country, but in practice, this is not always the case. Seek advice from the British consulate in your chosen country if you are unsure.

If you are looking for work
You can live in another EU member state for 3–6 months while looking for work. Again, we recommend that you always check with the authorities in your chosen country.

And remember, you can't be asked to leave at the end of this period if you can prove you have a realistic chance of finding a job. You might do this by pointing out that you still have interviews to attend.

Proof of health insurance and means of support while finding a job are essential, whether in the form of savings, a bequest or unemployment benefits paid to you while abroad. This is to prevent you becoming a burden on a country's social security system. Each country is free to set its own standards for what constitutes the means to support yourself. It is always advisable to check with the relevant embassy or consulate before you leave that you have adequate provision.

If you are a student

You will be issued with a residence permit if you wish to study in another EU country for more than three months. You will also need proof of health insurance and enough money to support yourself.

If you are retired

You can retire to any EU state, but proof of health insurance and the means to pay your way are essential.

What paperwork do I need to take?

The documents you need to apply for your residence permit will differ from country to country. To be on the safe side, check with the consulate of the country to which you are moving before you travel.

Members of your family who are EU nationals are also entitled to residence permits. Your family is defined as follows:

Your spouse: under EU law, your spouse is defined as your husband or wife. Individual

nations are free to make their own rules about whether this includes same-sex partners and couples who aren't married.

Your children: those aged under 21, or older if they are dependent on you.

Your parents and parents-in-law: provided they are dependent on you. (This does not apply to students.)

You will need to take proof of kinship, such as your marriage certificate, or your children's birth certificates.

Family members who are not EU nationals are also entitled to accompany you, however, they may need entry visas. Check with the embassy of the country you are going to before you leave, or grandma might face the nightmare of being refused entry. Relatives who aren't EU nationals will be issued with a different type of residence permit, also applied for from the relevant authorities when you reach your chosen country.

Can I be refused right of residence?

EU countries may refuse to issue or renew a residence permit under the following circumstances:

- If your behaviour constitutes a threat to public order or security. However, having a criminal record does not mean an automatic refusal. Each case is judged individually.
- If you have a disease that may jeopardize public health, such as cholera or smallpox.

If you are refused right of residence, you must be told why and given enough time to prepare a defence.

Your Possessions

You are entitled to move your personal property to another EU country without being taxed or paying customs duties. However, restrictions on goods such as arms and ammunition may be imposed, so if you're a gun enthusiast, you might have a spot of bother getting your stuff through customs.

Before you go
- Check electrical appliances for compatibility with the norms at your destination.
- Make sure you know how long it's going to take your belongings to arrive, and where you'll stay until they do.
- Get a full inventory of your possessions and include receipts or approximate values for each item in the local currency.

Your Pets

Get up-to-date vaccination certificates and other documents required for your animal(s).

Consider getting a pet passport if you are likely to be taking your animal back and forth. Information about this is available from your vet or specialist pet carriers.

Your Car

You can take your car into any other EU country. Eventually, however, you will have to register your vehicle with local plates. The period of grace involved varies from country to country, so consult the relevant embassy for details.

Your British or EU driving licence qualifies you to drive in any other state of the EU for as long as the licence is valid. However, the country you are moving to will have its own rules about medical checks and so on. It might also be necessary to register your driving licence. Contact the relevant local authority for details.

If you have a new private vehicle bought after 1 January 1996 in any EU country, your car is considered to be fine and dandy. However, if you purchased a second-hand car in an EU country other than your chosen place of residence, or your car pre-dates 1996, you may be asked to submit your vehicle to a roadworthiness test. The driving authority in your chosen country will be able to advise you.

Before you go
- Have your car serviced – you don't want it breaking down before you get to Calais.
- Make sure you have your vehicle registration document, MOT certificate, insurance papers and driving licence.
- Check that your insurance covers you and the car for the countries you will drive in.
- Contact the DVLA for any forms you might need, such as import applications.
- Ask your motoring organization or insurance company for details about what you are required to carry in your car, e.g. warning triangles, spare bulbs.

Get a Job

The good old EU helps you out yet again by simplifying the business of having your professional qualifications gained in one country recognized in another. It starts by dividing professions into three basic categories.

1. Unregulated professions
If your profession is not regulated in the country in which you wish to work, no official recognition of your qualifications is needed. You may begin work straight away.

2. EU-regulated professions
Qualifications for some professionals, such as doctors, vets, midwives, architects, pharmacists, nurses and dentists, have been coordinated throughout the EU. Your national qualifications will allow you to practise these professions in all EU countries.

3. Other professions
Professionals, such as lawyers, psychologists and engineers, must apply to the relevant authorities in their chosen country for their qualifications to be recognized. This may take several months, so apply in plenty of time. In some cases, you may be asked to undergo additional training or tests to make up differences between national standards.

Which applies to me?
Remember our mantra: check with the consulate or embassy before you go. Advice on recognition of professional qualifications can also be obtained from your trade association.

For further advice about job vacancies and working in other member states, European Employment Services (EURES) counsellors can be contacted through your local job centre. You can also access information online (see page 154).

What if I'm self-employed?
Unfortunately, you can't just stick up posters and start taking clients. You will be required to register with certain official bodies, which vary from country to country. Contact the relevant embassy for details.

Some self-employed people, such as hairdressers and construction workers, may need to hold a particular qualification, but the authorities are required to accept proof of a period of experience in your home nation as a substitute for the national qualification. Before you go you must apply to have your experience certified under the UK Certificates of Experience scheme. Contact the Department of Education and Skills (see page 154) for details.

Get Clued Up

What happens if you fall sick, get pregnant, lose your job or retire? Every country makes provision for all these eventualities, and it's in your interest to find out how.

Social security and welfare

When you begin work in another country in the EU, you are entitled to the same social security benefits as nationals. These include sickness, maternity, disability, old-age, death and unemployment benefits. Of course, you can't ride the bus without paying the fare, so you will have to make the same contributions as everyone else. You are also entitled to the same welfare benefits as nationals in the country where you work, including access to local authority housing. These benefits vary from country to country, so it is wise to apply for precise information from the embassy or consulate.

For more information go to the Foreign and Commonwealth Office website (see page 154) and search for benefits.

Pensions

If you are entitled to retirement benefits, you will receive them regardless of where you are living. All EU countries operate a system of totalization, whereby contributions made in one country qualify for pensions in another, so ensure all your contributions are taken into account when the authorities are deciding if you are entitled to a pension.

If you decide to retire abroad, you must inform the UK authorities that you are moving, tell them when you are going and give them a forwarding address.

Those you should inform are:
- Your private pension scheme provider
- Your local social security office
- The Inland Revenue National Insurance Contributions Office (International Services)
- The Department for Work and Pensions (DWP)

You must also let them know if you change your address while living abroad.

If you move to an EU country and you are entitled to a UK state retirement pension, long-term incapacity benefit, widow's benefits or bereavement benefit, you need form E121 from the DWP. You should be entitled to the same free or reduced-cost state medical treatment as a national pensioner in your country of residence.

We strongly advise that you get health insurance to cover private medical and dental treatment in your chosen country.

Grants

If you choose to study in another EU country, you must be paid the same grants as nationals to cover course fees (which can be hefty). However, this does not apply to maintenance grants; you will be required to pay your own living expenses. Occasionally, some countries, off their own backs, may decide to give grants or other forms of financial assistance to foreign students. Always check: you could be pleasantly surprised. Contact the embassy or consulate to see what's available. And, just on the off-chance, it is always worth contacting your local education authority to see if you are entitled to a scholarship or other financial support while studying abroad.

Academic qualifications

Academic awards from one member state are equivalent to those issued in another. This means that, in theory, you could take a first degree in one country, an MA in another and a PhD in a third.

For details of relevant national authorities for recognizing academic qualifications, see page 154.

Voting

Expatriates are entitled to vote in and stand as candidates in local and European Parliament elections, but not in national elections.

Some countries allow you to vote in local elections in your country of origin as well as your country of residence. However, you have only one vote to elect a member of the European Parliament.

Enforcing your rights

If you feel you have been treated unfairly, there are many ways of raising your case. First go through the usual national procedures, such as courts and tribunals. If you still aren't happy, you can enforce your rights at EU level. The first thing to try is the European Commission. If it considers that you have a case and EU law has been infringed, it can demand an explanation from the authority concerned. If the Commission is not satisfied with the response, it can take further action.

You can also raise your case with an MEP, or petition the European Parliament (see page 154).

In cases of maladministration by EU institutions, you can take your case to the European Ombudsman (see page 154).

France

The French call their country *La Belle France* (Beautiful France), and, like all things beautiful, it can be entrancing, frustrating, elusive and compelling in equal measure.

The people are charming and aloof, proud and diffident, full of contradictions. Legend has it that Frenchmen are great lovers and lousy husbands. And how do you reconcile the statistics that suggest less than half the French bathe every day, and yet they spend more on beauty products than any other country in the world?

Maybe it's best not even to try to understand them, and instead just sit back and enjoy what they've got to offer, which is the French way of life. And be it rustic and rural or metropolitan and sophisticated, there will always be good food, fine wine and a certain *je ne sais quoi*.

The topography of France is as hard to pin down as its character. From the dramatic mountains of the Alps to the elegant chateaux of the Loire valley, from the farms and villages of Provence to the rugged coastline of Brittany, France has been blessed with stunning countryside that, by European standards, is sparsely populated. It has the same population as Britain with a land mass twice the size.

Sixty per cent of France is used for agriculture, and the French remain a nation obsessed with the land. So, despite the sophistication of Paris and the Côte d'Azure, France remains in essence a rural country. Each region has its own food, wines and traditions, which are celebrated and preserved for future generations. Nowhere is this more evident than in the cuisine: from the crêpes and seafood of Brittany to the olives and tomatoes of Provence, it is varied, robust, surprising and unique.

Alongside the traditional cuisine are ethnic foods from Africa, the Caribbean, Indo-China, the Pacific and the Middle East, all reflecting both France's colonial heritage and its multicultural present.

Politics

France is composed of 22 administrative regions (*régions*) divided into 96 *départements* (roughly equivalent to counties), which are further subdivided into districts, municipalities and cantons. All these areas, together with the overseas *départements* and territories, constitute the French Republic.

The Fifth French Republic is governed under a constitution adopted in 1958. It provides a strong president, directly elected to a five-year term of office, and has a parliament consisting of two chambers: the National Assembly, composed of 577 deputies, each elected by popular vote every five years; and the Senate, made up of 317 senators, voted for by the electoral college, who hold office for nine years and are renewed one third at a time.

The influence of conservative Charles de Gaulle (president from 1954 to 1968) cannot be underestimated. He doggedly insisted on independence from the United States and NATO in military affairs, and French mistrust of the USA continues to this day.

France remained basically conservative for nearly 30 years, until 1981, when a socialist, François Mitterrand, was elected president and embarked on a programme that included administrative decentralization and nationalization of banks and industry – the opposite of what Margaret Thatcher was doing at the time in Britain.

Rising unemployment and other economic difficulties, as well as corruption scandals, led to a socialist defeat in 1993. The rest of the decade was characterized by an uneasy cohabitation between the socialists and conservatives, until 2002, when socialist Lionel Jospin lost the presidential election. At the same time, a far right candidate qualified for the second round – a sign of growing racial tensions. Amid much national soul-searching, the moderate right-winger Jacques Chirac eventually won by more than 80% of the vote. Conservatives also won the majority of seats in the National Assembly.

Economy

France is one of the world's major economic powers. It is also a strongly agricultural nation, and the second largest producer of wine (only Italy makes more). Major industrial products include chemicals, textiles, steel, food, motor vehicles and aircraft. Tourism is important, as is the production of luxury goods, such as perfume. The railways, utilities, many banks and some key industries are nationalized, but there has been some recent movement towards privatization.

If you happen to be a nuclear scientist, France could be the place for you. It has the world's second largest number of operating nuclear power plants, which, in 2002, produced over 75% of its electricity.

France is the only European country where public workers have an unlimited right to strike – and we all know they use it. Direct action also extends to other sectors. French farmers and lorry drivers, for example, are notorious for taking to the streets and autoroutes to protect their interests.

Currency

The French have embraced the euro, but there have been complaints that prices have risen as a result.

Religion

Roman Catholicism is the dominant religion in France, although church attendance is low. Four million Muslims, mostly of North-African descent (from the wave of immigration that took place during the 1950s and 1960s), now live in France, making Islam the second biggest religion in the country. The next main group is Protestants, followed by Jews (France has the largest Jewish population in Europe).

Time difference

France is on Central European Time, which is one hour ahead of GMT. Daylight Saving Time from the last Sunday in March to the last Sunday in October is two hours ahead of GMT (one hour ahead of British Summer Time).

Climate

Like so much about France, the climate is hard to put a finger on. In the northwest it is warm and wet; in the northeast the winters are cold and the summers hot. Meanwhile, the Alps are permanently topped with snow, yet the southern coastal plains rarely see frost, and even rain is scarce during the summer.

Brits in France

There are an estimated 100,000 to 150,000 British people living in France. Unlike expats in Spain, who have formed their own distinct communities, those in France usually show every sign of wanting to integrate into French life and take an active part in the existing community.

Love/Hate

'Sitting outside a café having a croissant and coffee has got to be one of the greatest pleasures of living in France.'

'It's obvious, but the food is just amazing. They take it so much more seriously than we do. Meals are prepared with pride and are an integral part of life.'

'I love shopping in the local market. It is so much more satisfying buying direct from the producer than from a supermarket where everything is uniform, sterile and vacuum-packed.'

'The French – I think they're great – sardonic, bolshie, voluble and emotional. You just need to learn not to take them at face value. A gruff exterior can hide a wonderfully warm future friend.'

'The weather has made such a difference to the health of the whole family. We're all outside so much more. The TV is not on half as much. We'll sit outside and have long lunches where we actually talk to each other.'

'If you don't speak the language, you can feel very isolated and it can seem as if the French people are just not trying to understand you.'

'The taxi drivers are so unfriendly, they never know where they're going and inevitably take you the longest way round possible.'

'Dog poo! It's everywhere. The notion that it's far more sociable to clear it up just hasn't caught on here yet.'

'The bureaucracy. It's an art form. You need to be very, very patient.'

'The work culture is quite different. You can't underestimate the importance of relationships. You need to go for coffee, get to know people, make friends with them. It's the only way you'll get things done. People only do what you ask if they know you. The fact it's their job isn't enough. People do things when they think it ought to be done rather than when you ask them to.'

Get There

As with all EU countries, there is nothing to stop you getting up and going off to France at any time. Practically, of course, the reality is a little different, and there is still (surprise, surprise) bureaucracy to contend with.

All you need for the first three months of living in France is a valid passport. But if you intend to live there permanently, or to work for more than three months, you should apply for a *carte de séjour* (residence permit). This allows you to live and work in France, is valid for ten years and is automatically renewable.

Children do not need a *carte de séjour* until they are 16, when they must apply for it within a month of their birthday. However, cards are sometimes issued for safety reasons to under-16s (at their parents' request) if they are travelling alone outside France, or without a member of their immediate family.

There are three different categories of *carte de séjour*:

Actif: For those who are working. You will need to show a copy of your employment contract.
Non-actif: For those retired or not working. You will need to show proof of means of support.
Étudiant: For students. You will need proof that you are enrolled at a French school, college or university.

Getting your *carte de séjour*

You must apply within three months of arrival at the *Service des Etrangers* at the *préfecture* (police station) of the *département*, or the *mairie* (town hall) where you live. It is a good idea to go in person in case any problems arise. If you have all the relevant documents, it should take only one trip, but don't count on it; some town hall jobsworths seem to delight in making the process as painful as possible.

Keep photocopies of all your documents just in case anything goes astray.

You will need...

- Three passport photographs taken against a light background
- Passport
- Birth certificate and marriage certificate, if applicable
- Contract of employment, if applicable
- An electricity (EDF) bill with your name and address, *or* a copy of the *acte de vente* (deed of sale) if you have bought a house in France, *or*, if you are renting, a receipt for rent paid (*quittance de loyer*)
- An E111 form or some other document as proof of social security/health care cover.

Citizenship

Contact the British Embassy in France (see page 154) for details.

Pets

Britain's rabies-free status means that there are few problems in taking pets to France, but always check with your vet and the French Embassy for the latest situation and vaccination requirements.

Attacks by certain types of dog have led to some breeds being banned from importation. These include pit bull terriers, English mastiffs or Staffordshire bull terrier crosses, and purebreeds without Kennel Club registration and papers.

Your car

The French customs service (*Direction des Douanes*) is your first port of call for up-to-date information about bringing a British-registered car into France. There is a local customs office in every main town in France, and information and forms are available on the Internet (see page 155). The DVLA (see page 154) is also a good source of information, and can tell you which forms you will need.

Your UK driving licence will be valid in France for a year before you have to exchange it for a French one. The French legal age for driving is 18, so if you are 17 and have passed your test in the UK, your licence will not be valid until your eighteenth birthday.

Before you leave for France, make sure you have prepared your car as recommended in the EU section (see pages 36–7).

When you're there

- After a certain period of time (see EU section, page 36) you must register your car with the *préfecture de police* in the area you live to get a *carte grise* (grey card).
- The *numéro d'immatriculation* on the *carte grise* is the registration number. You can get plates made at almost any petrol station.

Other belongings

There are no restrictions on taking your household goods from one EU country to another. However, it is always wise to have a detailed inventory that includes receipts or approximate values in case customs officers decide to give you a hard time.

One word of warning – if it is likely that your removal lorry might block a street at your destination, make sure you inform the *préfecture*. If the police have not been informed and traffic is affected, you could be fined.

Most British electrical appliances work in France; you'll just need to buy an adapter or change the plug. British televisions and radios won't work, however, so you'll have to buy them when you get there.

Get a Home

France is a house-lover's paradise. Property prices have traditionally been far lower than the UK, and there is a seemingly endless supply of charmingly run-down *gîtes*, cottages, farmhouses, *moulins* and chateaux just begging to be loved, restored and turned into money-spinning B&Bs, auberges or holiday lets.

Of course, buying property is never entirely straightforward, and the French system can be about as clear as mud to outsiders, so do ensure you use someone who knows the system, who you can communicate with properly, who will translate the legal documents if necessary and generally make sure your interests are taken care of.

Unlike the UK, France does not consider it necessary for the buyer and seller to have different lawyers. The legalities are handled by a *notaire* (solicitor), whose job is to make sure the sale is procedurally and legally correct.

He is not there to act on behalf of either party. So if your French is less than perfect and you want some hand-holding, make sure you appoint your own *notaire*, or get in touch with one of the many estate agents who specializes in the expat sector. He or she will be able to give you advice on all aspects of the sale.

It may seen premature, but this is also the time to ask about French inheritance law. Unlike the UK, which allows you to choose who will inherit your assets, France has strict laws safeguarding the rights of your children or blood relatives to a share of your estate. If you buy property in France, it will be subject to these laws. This can lead to a number of tricky situations. For example, if a husband dies and one or more of the children is under 18, his wife will not be able to sell the property without the permission of a French court acting on behalf of her underage child. This is time-consuming and expensive. If the deceased has no children, parents and siblings may also have a claim on the estate.

The time to sort this out is before buying, as the form of the contract will dictate what happens should you die.

Before you go

- Do some serious house-hunting. France is easy and cheap to get to, so it's feasible to do lots of research.
- Look on the Internet for companies specializing in French property (see page 154). Some French property companies have offices in the UK and can help you with methods of finance, as well as finding your ideal home.

Mainland Europeans have far fewer hang-ups about home-owning than Britons, who regard 'getting on the property ladder' as something of a Holy Grail. Perhaps it's because we live our lives behind our 'castle' walls, whereas our European counterparts, with better weather and better food, tend to live theirs in the cafés and streets, and think renting forever is perfectly OK. Who knows? In fact, it must be said that renting is a very good idea – particularly if you are finding your feet in a new country. The rural idyll that seems so attractive from your semi in Surbiton may not be so appealing when you have to negotiate pot-holes, ford a river and speak very nicely to a Limousin bull just to pick up the paper.

Another bonus of renting is that it can give you breathing space to find jobs, apply for residency, brush up your language skills and generally get to grips with the French psyche before tackling the many-headed monster that is house buying in France. You really do have to be on your toes, so 'Buyer beware' should be your mantra, and we recommend that you check and double-check absolutely everything.

Renting or buying, whichever you choose, remember always to seek professional advice.

Renting

The French have embraced the Internet wholeheartedly when it comes to property, and there is a whole host of sites dedicated to getting landlords and tenants together. Some may charge a subscription fee, but it can be worth the price for the time saved.

Whereas in the UK it is usually the landlord who pays the estate agent commission for letting a property, in France estate agents also charge the tenant a fee, which can be as high as a month's rent. Little wonder, then, that people try to bypass this by looking on the Internet and scanning the classified ads (*De particuler à particuler*) in the local newspaper.

An estate agent or landlord will need to see three recent payslips to confirm that your monthly salary is at least three times the monthly rent.

Rental contracts in France are governed by a law that dictates:

- If the property is owned by a company, the minimum lease is six years.
- The minimum lease is three years if owned by an individual, and the landlord cannot give the tenant notice during this time.
- If the property is rented by a company, they must give three months' notice.
- If the property is rented by an individual, he or she must give a month's notice.
- The tenant has right of renewal when the lease is up.
- The owner cannot ask for more than two months' rent as a deposit.
- Rent increases will probably be added once a year on the date you signed your contract. By law your landlord can increase your rent only by a figure linked to costs in the building trade, usually up to 4% a year. Rent increases are made at your landlord's discretion.

Your rent (*loyer*) also includes charges to cover the cost of such things as employing a concierge (caretaker), cleaning of communal areas and, perhaps, heating.

Note: If the property needs work done to it, you might be able to negotiate a few weeks rent-free in return for doing it yourself.

Property tax

Once you have signed your contract, you need to go to your local town hall to register. You will then be liable for *taxe d'habitation* (housing tax), which is the French equivalent of council tax and, like its UK counterpart, varies according to where you live. However, unlike the UK, you pay according to where you are living on 1 January of each year.

Insurance

The tenant is responsible for buildings insurance, and you must provide the landlord with proof of insurance every year. If something happens, the insurer pays the landlord on your behalf.

Many insurance companies offer information on their websites (see page 154).

The infamous concierge

If you live in a block of apartments, it's a good idea to make friends with the concierge. Those who hold this post have a reputation for being surly, nosy and generally unhelpful, but they can be your best friend in the early days of life in a new town or city. They will undoubtedly know a fair bit about the local area, and be able to help if you have a problem, such as needing a plumber.

With that in mind, don't forget that it is traditional to give gifts to the concierge at New Year. The amount varies, so check with your neighbours, but it likely to be in the region of 10% of the monthly rent.

Buying

There are three main pieces of advice to heed before you start: be prepared; take advice; and don't expect it to be quick.

Estate agents in France are qualified and registered, unlike those in the UK, and will have a *carte professionelle* to show you. When you first visit an agent you may be asked to sign a *bon de visite*. This is nothing to worry about, it simply covers the agent by stating that he or she is entitled to the vendor's commission if he makes a sale.

A *mandat de recherche* (instruction to research) is an agreement between you and the agent for him or her to look for property on your behalf. This is a formal arrangement as you are directly engaging the agent's services and will be expected to pay commission if they find you a property. Sometimes you can be charged even if they do not come up with the goods, so beware.

The procedures for buying a property in France can vary according to the type of place you want. A vineyard or farm, for example, will be subject to different procedures and costs than a typical house. But in general the process will follow three stages.

1. The initial contract

When you have found your little piece of French perfection, your first move is to negotiate an initial agreement with the seller. If this is drawn up by an estate agent, it is called a *sous-seing privé*. If it is drawn up by a *notaire*, it is called a *compromis de vente*. Other forms of preliminary contract exist, but they are less common.

Whichever method you use to draw up your initial contract, it is legally binding. You will then be required to pay a deposit of up to 10% of the purchase price to the *notaire*. If you renege on the agreement (for reasons other than not being able to get a mortgage),

you will lose your deposit. Once the contract has been signed, the property is taken off the market.

The contract will have a completion date – traditionally 60 days from the date of signing – but the *notaire*'s checks can take longer, so you should not rely on this being the actual date you get the keys.

Before signing

- A European lawyer or your own *notaire* (a solicitor who does contractual work, such as wills and house contracts) will be able to give you advice. The duty of the public *notaire* is to the State; it is not his role to advise either party.
- Check the document carefully and get it translated if necessary.
- Surveys are not a usual part of the buying process in France. The bank will usually take a *hypothèque* (warranty) on the property, and it's up to you to ask

individual workmen about what needs doing and how much it will cost. This should inform your offer price. There is nothing to stop you getting a survey, but it would be seen as unusual.

- Make checks at the local town hall for any proposed development in the area. You don't want to lose your stunning views to property developers or road builders shortly after moving in.
- Check *exactly* what is included in the sale. Are all the outbuildings part of the package? What about land, boundaries and fixtures and fittings? (It has been known for fitted kitchens to be removed.) Is the estate agent's commission to be paid by the vendor or is it included in the price? All these should be cleared up *before* you sign the *sous-seing privé* or *compromis de vente*.
- Remember, never give your deposit to the seller, it should always go to the *notaire*.

2. The *notaire*'s checks

Once the documents for stage 1 have been signed, the independent *notaire* will check whether there are any issues that could affect the legality of the sale, such as outstanding charges, third-party rights of way, or claim on the property by the local authority. This will take between six and eight weeks. In the meantime, you have time to sort out finances for the purchase. (Failure to get a mortgage is an obligatory suspensive clause, so you won't be penalized if you can't get one.) You might also choose to get advice on the inheritance situation at this stage: after signature of the final deed, it is too late.

3. The *acte de vente*

The final stage is the actual exchange of contracts, which takes place in person at the *notaire's* office. You pay the *notaire*

the balance and he passes it on to the seller. You will also have to pay legal and registration fees, which are usually about 7% of the purchase price.

French law dictates that if you have a mortgage, you must also have a life assurance policy approved by the lender to cover the loan, so make sure this is in place by your completion date. Also ensure that you have buildings and contents insurance so you are covered as soon as the property becomes yours.

Before signing, the *notaire* will need:

- The balance of the purchase price, including legal fees and registration taxes
- A copy of your birth certificate (and marriage certificate, if applicable) translated into French.

Additional costs

Apart from the 7% charge for legal and registration fees, an additional fee must be paid to the *notaire* if you are taking out a mortgage. This is usually 1 or 2% of the loan value. You will also need to budget for the mortgage arrangement fee. Purchases are also subject to VAT:

- A house and the first 2,500 square metres at between 8% and 10%
- Agricultural land to be cultivated at 16.2%
- Agricultural land not to be cultivated 18.2%
- Building land up to 2,500 square metres 20.6%

Property taxes

As a home-owner, you will be liable for *taxe foncière* (land tax). This is payable on 1 January each year, but, unlike *taxe d'habitation*, which is paid by whoever is living in the property on 1 January for the whole year, this can be divided according to how long each party has owned the property. This needs to be made clear in the contract.

Mortgages

The largest mortgage lender in France is Crédit Agricole. Several UK high-street lenders have French sections and expert advisers who can outline the different ways of financing property abroad, including offshore accounts and releasing equity from your UK home. Your lender will also outline the factors to consider when deciding how to pay your mortgage. Fluctuating exchange rates and the cost of changing large amounts of money from sterling into euros can both significantly damage your financial health and need to be taken into account. There are also numerous UK-based mortgage brokers who specialize in French mortgages and can guide you through the system, including putting you in touch with English-speaking *notaires* or estate agents.

How large a mortgage can I get?

By law the lender must make sure you can afford the repayments, so, as a rule of thumb, mortgage payments cannot exceed 30% of your net income.

The total loan for non-resident borrowers is usually no more than 80% of the valuation (not necessarily what you pay for it). For second homes this could drop to 50%, so make sure you have an adequate pot of money to cover your deposit. If you are resident in France you will not need so much. Although 100% mortgages are rare, they are possible.

How is income calculated?

Your income can include spouse's income and sometimes that of a third person.

What if I'm not employed?

Foreigners who are self-employed or retired with no proof of fixed income might have trouble getting a mortgage. Self-employed applicants will need to show accounts for at least the last three years. Your income will be calculated as the average of these three years.

When do I arrange a mortgage?

Usually you get your mortgage once the first stage of the buying process is complete, but it is possible to arrange a mortgage in advance, which will set a maximum loan amount and is subject to the bank's valuation of the property. It is usually valid for 8–12 weeks.

How long will it take?

It will take a couple of weeks to get your loan approved. The 24-hour mortgage has yet to find favour in France. Once your application has been approved, there is a ten-day 'cooling off' period. When that is up, you have 30 days to accept the mortgage.

Are there any charges?

There are fees to be paid both to the lending bank and to the *notaire* for registering the mortgage on the property:

- *Notaire*'s fee: 1–2% of the mortgage value
- Bank's fees: 1% of mortgage value
- Valuation cost

These fees cannot be covered by the mortgage, so make sure you have accounted for this from your savings and/or deposit.

What types of mortgage are available?

There are two main types of French mortgage.

Variable rate mortgages are linked to the Central Bank variations in interest rates. They can be converted into fixed rate mortgages at a later date and there are not usually any redemption penalties. When interest rates change it is not the monthly payment that changes, but the length of the mortgage. There is also a capped variable rate.

Fixed rate mortgages have the interest rate fixed for the entire term of the mortgage, so you always know exactly how much you will have to pay. There are early redemption penalties and you are not able to switch to a variable rate later on.

Connecting utilities

Electricité de France (EDF) is the national electricity supplier. To open a new account you should call your local office and give the name of your property's previous occupant. The EDF will come and read the meter and set up a new account. The account number will be on your first bill, which will have two main components: the subscription and the energy consumed. There are a number of tariff options and rates, depending on your consumption. The company prefers payment by direct debit.

Gaz de France (GDF), a nationalized company linked to EDF, handles the gas supply. The procedure for opening an account and paying bills is similar to that for electricity.

Water is supplied locally by private companies. Bills are payable quarterly by the usual means. Contact your local water company to arrange a contract.

France Télécom (FT) supplies telephone lines. Dial 1014 from a public phone to find your local office. You may be asked if there is an existing phone socket on the property, and for the name and phone number of the property's previous occupant, so try to find out this information before you apply. If there isn't already a socket, the first two are usually installed for free. You will have to pay for the line installation and setting up the phone number, but will be given the option of renting or buying the phone. The company requires you to present proof of identification, such as a passport, and proof of address, such as a lease or EDF bill.

Telephone bills are sent every two months. The peak rate is Monday to Friday, 8 a.m. to 7 p.m. The reduced rate is Monday to Friday, 7 p.m. to 8 a.m. and all day Saturday and Sunday.

TV licence

You need a television licence in France. When you buy or rent a TV, the shop will send your details to the TV licence office. You will receive a bill annually.

Get a Job

Although France is the world's fourth largest economic power according to GDP, unemployment is among the highest in Europe, and significantly higher than in the UK.

Of course, the better qualified you are and the better you speak the language, the higher your chances of getting a decent job. In fact, if you do not speak French, you need to start learning, or it will seriously hinder your chances of making a living. French employers won't take you seriously, and the majority of French officials won't understand you.

Before you go

- Don't forget to check whether your qualifications are recognized in France. For further information about this, see the EU section, page 37.
- Make a few reconnaissance trips. Nothing can replace face-to-face contact, and many jobs come through networking rather than advertisements.
- Your local Job Centre can give you advice about finding a job in Europe and whether you can continue to claim Job Seeker's Allowance for a time while you are there.
- Log on to the website of the EURES job-listing service (see page 154).

- Prepare a CV and keep it brief (two pages maximum).

Once you arrive
There are several tried-and-tested places to find jobs advertised.

Newspapers and specialist magazines are the obvious place to start. Most newspapers devote different days to particular job sectors, so find out which is the one for you. Many French newspapers also have online editions (see page 155).

You can also place your own advertisement in national or local French newspapers, or in the Paris edition of the *International Herald Tribune* through their London office (see page 154).

Recruitment agencies can advise on every aspect of your career, from suitable jobs to salary expectations. Although many have websites, it is better to make personal contact. For a selection of recruitment specialists see page 155.

Internet sites run by recruitment and temping agencies are many and various. You can register and post your CV with them, and also see their lists of job vacancies.

The British Chamber of Commerce in France can supply you with a list of British companies operating in the country. It also offers information about starting your own business, and has a monthly review in which you can place classified ads (see page 154).

ANPE (*Agence Nationale Pour l'Emploi*) is the French employment service. You can register with it once you arrive.

Applying for jobs
It is always good practice to keep CVs brief – two pages maximum – and to highlight your relevant experience. An accompanying letter should emphasize your suitable qualities for the job.

A peculiarity of France is that the vast majority of employers prefer the letter to be handwritten. Graphology is widely used as a recruitment tool, and good handwriting is taken as a sign of good education.

Employment contracts
There are three types of employment contract, and the type you get will depend on how long you are contracted for.

Contrat de Travail Temporaire (CTT) – temporary employment contract
Contrat à Durée Déterminée (CDD) – short/fixed-term contract
Contrat à Durée Indéterminée (DDI) – permanent contract

The *code du travail* (work code of practice) governs general legal obligations for all employers. There is then a *convention du travail* (work agreement), which is specific to the sector or industry you work in.

The legal working week is 35 hours, equivalent to 1,600 hours per year. Anything more than that constitutes overtime, and holiday or extra pay must be given at a rate of 125% for more than 35 hours, and 150% after 44 hours. Annual holiday (excluding the 11 public holidays) is a minimum of five weeks. Information about working time regulation in France is available online (see page 155).

The minimum wage (*Salaire Minimum Interprofessionnel de Croissance*, or SMIC) is €1215.11 per month.

Further information about working in France is available from the *Ministre d'Emploi et Solidarité* (Ministry for Social Affairs, Labour and Solidarity), see page 155.

Get Healthy

The French health service is regarded by many as the best in the world, so you couldn't be in a better place to get treatment. Employers pay heavy health taxes, and the self-employed must have health insurance.

Medical costs are paid by the patient and then reclaimed from the health service, *Caisse Primaire d'Assurance Maladie* (CPAM). Repayments might cover only 75% of the costs, so most people take out extra insurance to fill the gap.

Your E111 will entitle you to health care for a limited period, but you should get into the French system as soon as possible.

Social Health Care insurance in France covers four out of five residents for medical costs arising from illness, pregnancy, disability and death. A second plan covers accidents at work and occupational diseases.

Getting into the French health system

To get access to the full range of services available through the French health service you first need a *numéro de sécurité sociale* (social security number) so you can make contributions. Your employer will apply for this on your behalf by completing a *declaration unique d'embauche* (declaration of employment), which must be faxed to the *Union pour le Recouvrement des cotisations de la Sécurité Sociale et des Allocations Familiales* (URSSAF) and registered with the local social security centre, which will give you a temporary number, later replaced with a permanent one. You will then receive a document with your insurance details and a *carte vitale* (vital card), which is like a credit card and has a chip containing your relevant details, enabling you to reclaim the cost of treatment. If you are not working, ask about *couverture maladie universelle* (universal health insurance) at your local social security centre.

Eligibility

To benefit from the French health system you must have made a minimum number of contributions or have worked a minimum number of hours. If you have a regular income, your payments will be deducted from your salary, just as it is the UK. If you don't have a regular income, you should send payslips to URSSAF once a year showing that you have worked at least 60 hours or earned at least 60 times the hourly basic minimum wage. If you don't work, you are still covered if you are the child, spouse or de facto partner of someone who is making contributions.

How it works

The patient is free to consult the health professional of their choice, be it GP, specialist, dentist or nurse. However, the system is not free at the point of delivery. It works on the principle that the patient pays up front. The government will then reimburse the agreed subsidy. The balance may be covered by private health insurance if you have it, so it really pays to keep on top of your paperwork.

The exception to this rule is emergency hospital treatment, which does not need to be paid for in advance. If you show your *carte vitale*, the subsidy will be taken into account and you will pay only the difference, not the full price.

Expect a visit to the GP (*médecin généraliste*) to cost about €17.50 without a discount, and €12 with your *carte vitale*.

Although the French health-care system is one of the best in the world, it is worth bearing in mind that, as with many other aspects of life overseas, you need to have some financial back up to see you through whilst you deal with all the necessary bureaucracy. Peter Maslen, who relocated to France in series 1 with his wife Anna and children, Bethany and Joseph, found that entering the French health-care system was not as easy as it first seemed:

'You have to get a French social security number to register for French health insurance and to apply you have to show you have the financial means to support yourself. But I couldn't work until we had attended a course, called a stage, in how to set up a business. You can't even buy top-up health insurance without a social security number. If you haven't got a job after three months you are in limbo – neither system will cover you. We weren't covered for about seven months. In that time we ended up in casualty a couple of times with the inevitable bumps that kids get. It cost us about €200 (around £145). You really must come with savings in the bank.'

Types of health care

There are three types of health-care provider, and how much you pay will depend on who you choose to go to.

- Medical practitioners who have signed agreements with CPAM have fixed fees.
- Other practitioners are authorized to exceed these fees, but CPAM will not increase the subsidy, so the patient pays the increased cost.
- Private practitioners who have no agreement with CPAM must be paid for in full by the patient or their private health insurance.

Private health care

Government subsidies for certain expensive aspects of health care, such as dentistry and optometry, are negligible (€2–€3), so many people get private health insurance to cover the additional expenditure.

Hospitals

In an emergency go to casualty (*urgences*) at your nearest hospital (*hôpital*).

Pharmacies

Pharmacies, indicated by a green or red cross, are open during normal shopping hours. Details of the nearest 24-hour pharmacy will be displayed on the door.

Prescriptions must be paid for by the patient, but you can then apply to the CPAM for a partial refund, depending on your financial circumstances. If you have a serious condition that needs long-term treatment, you will probably be entitled to a full exemption certificate.

Get Wealthy

This section fills you in on handling your finances in France, covering everything from banks and bills to taxes and wills.

Banks
There are two types of banks in France – co-ops and commercial banks.

Co-ops, such as Crédit Agricole, have all the facilities and services of a national bank, but their local branches are run independently. As an account holder, you have the option of buying shares. If you have a mortgage, you will have to buy a certain number of shares in the branch. Commercial banks offer all the same services, but can be more efficient than co-ops and offer a more personal service.

Opening a bank account
Opening a bank account is easy, and you do not need to be a resident to do it.

You will need…
- Proof of identity, such as a passport or driving licence
- Proof of address, such as a utility bill or rental agreement

If you do have difficulty opening an account (perhaps you haven't got a fixed address yet), try *La Poste* (the Post Office), who can offer you the equivalent of a post-office account.

Once you have your bank account details (*relevé d'identité bancaire*), you can set up direct debits and standing orders. It will take approximately two weeks for your cheque book and *carte bleue* (cheque, debit or cashpoint card) to come through. It is a criminal offence to write a cheque if you do not have the funds to cover it. Visa and Eurocard/Mastercard are the most popular credit cards in France, and will cost you between €23 and €37 a year. You will need your PIN number when paying by credit card.

Cheques
The French write their cheques differently from us – the amount in words comes first, then the name of the person or company to whom it's payable.

Cheque guarantee cards are not used in France, so you will have to present an official piece of ID, such as a driving licence or passport, if you pay for purchases by cheque.

Withdrawing cash
You can cash a cheque at your own branch by making it payable to yourself and producing an official piece of ID. You can also withdraw money from cash machines.

Bank charges and bank statements
Charges are levied much as they are in the UK, and statements are issued quarterly, unless you request them more frequently.

Banking hours
In general, banks are open Monday to Friday, 9 a.m. to 4 p.m., but some stay open until 5 p.m. Those open on Saturday may be closed on Monday.

Taxes
From this side of the Channel, we constantly hear stories of the superior French rail services, their modern, well-maintained roads and the excellence of their health-care system. It's true, the services can be better, but you pay handsomely for them. Income tax and social security take a large chunk of your earnings.

The tax year runs from 1 January to 31 December, and you have to submit a return even if you have no tax to pay. The form will be sent to you in February and you must have completed it by mid-March. In the first year, you will be sent a tax bill in August, which you have to pay by 15 September. In subsequent years, you will be asked to pay instalments in February and May on the basis of the tax you paid in the previous year.

If you disagree with the calculation of your tax bill, you can complain to the head of the local tax office. If your complaint is rejected, you may take your case to the tribunal or court mentioned in the rejection decision (*tribunal administratif* or *tribunal de grande instance*, depending on the tax involved).

Seek professional advice from an experienced tax adviser (*expert comptable* or *conseiller fiscal*) to avoid paying tax in both the UK and France.

Here are some of the taxes most likely to affect you.

Income tax (*Impôt sur le revenu*)

You will have to pay tax in France under the following circumstances:

- You spend 183 days or more in France in one year.
- Your permanent home or principal residence is in France.
- Your main source of income, investment or business is in France.

French income tax is progressive, which means that the more you earn, the more you pay. But a wide range of rebates and exemptions means that your actual rate may end up lower than it at first appears.

The most obvious example is the *quotient familial* (family quota), where the family is divided into 'units' and given allowances according to its size. For example, a single person is one unit; a couple represents two units and has the total income divided between them; the first two children each represent half a unit, and subsequent children a whole unit.

Wealth tax (*Impôt sur la fortune*)

A standard rate of wealth tax or a tax on property is applicable to French residents. The current qualifying rate is €720,000. French residents are taxed on assets owned in and outside France, while non-residents are taxed on assets in France only.

Capital gains tax (*Taxe des plus-values*)

This is a complicated area. Capital gains is charged on second or holiday homes. It diminishes the longer you have owned the property, reaching nil at 32 years. If you move frequently, doing up properties, you may be classified as a developer and charged tax at 50%, so make sure you take professional advice.

Land tax (*Taxe foncière*)

A tax is payable by all property owners on 1 January each year (see page 49).

Council tax (*Taxe d'habitation*)

This charge for local services is paid by whoever is living in the property on 1 January.

Value added tax (*Taxe sur la valeur ajoutée*)

VAT is already included in the price of goods in shops, and there are two different rates: 5.5% on basic foodstuffs, 19.6% on everything else.

Social security

Anyone living and working in France must join the French social security system, *Sécurité Sociale*, which covers pensions, benefits and health care. If you are working, your employer should register you automatically. Refer to the EU section (page 38) for further details.

Pensions

When you start work in France you will automatically pay contributions into the French state pension scheme. Refer to the EU section (page 38) for further details.

Retirement age in France is 60 for both men and women. To receive a full pension you must have contributed for 40 years. As in all countries, it is wise not to rely on the state pension alone, but to pay into a private scheme, too.

Tax break

Anyone living in France with two or more dependent children is eligible for *allocations familiales*. This is an allowance paid regardless of income, provided the mother is resident in France. Once a child is six years old, you will have to supply proof that they are enrolled in school.

For information contact the local *Caisse d'Allocations Familiales* (see phone book).

Wills

French inheritance law is complex and quite different from British law, which allows you to give whatever you like to whomever you like. The first thing you should do is seek advice and make sure there are no conflicts with your British will.

In France your legal heirs have inalienable rights to a certain percentage (*reserve légale*) of your French estate. The remainder (*quotité disponible*) can be given away as a lifetime gift or in a will.

The first surprise is that your husband or wife is not a legal heir and has no right to the *reserve légale* part of the estate. Your children have first call. If you have one child, you cannot give away more than half of your estate to someone else; two children, and this reduces to a third; three or more, and it is down to a quarter. If you have no children,

other family members, such as parents, brothers or sisters, may qualify as legal heirs.

There are ways of legally avoiding French inheritance law (though not the taxes) when buying property, such as buying through a company called a *société civile immobilière* (SCI) or inserting a *clause tontine* in the deeds. Both are complex and need careful advice and consideration.

A lifetime gift (from the *quotité disponible*) will be subject to gift tax (*droit de donation*), and on your death your French estate will be subject to succession tax (*droit de succession*). Again this is a complex area, so advice should be sought.

Get Wise

Education in France is compulsory from ages six to sixteen. There is a thriving private sector, mostly run by the Catholic Church, alongside state-run schools. About one-fifth of French pupils go to private schools.

International and British schools do exist, but are concentrated in Paris. A list of English-speaking and bilingual schools is available online from the British Council (see page 155).

To enrol your children in a primary or secondary French school, go to the local town hall or the *département* education office, or contact one of the addresses on page 155.

France's education system

Here's a quick rundown of what you can expect to encounter when you dip a toe into France's education system.

Nursery (*Halte-garderie*)

French nurseries are heavily oversubscribed, so if you are likely to be returning to work soon after giving birth, you should enrol your child while you're still in the early stages of pregnancy. The local town hall will have a list of nurseries in your area.

Pre-school, ages 3–6 (*Ecole maternelle*)
State-run pre-school groups introduce children to the school environment, and most French children attend one.

Primary school, ages 6–10 (*Ecole primaire*)
There are three stages in primary education:
- *Cours Préparatoire* (CP)
- *Cours Elémentaire* (CE 1 and 2, or tenth and ninth years)
- *Cours Moyen* (CM 1 and 2, or eighth and seventh years)

Note that the years are the reverse of those in the UK: tenth year is the lowest, and the first year the highest.

Collège, ages 11–14 (sixth to third years)
This is the first stage of secondary school. At the end of this stage, students sit the *Brevet des Collèges*, a public exam like the GCSE. It is not a formal entry examination to *lycée* (grammar school), but the result of it and a report are used to determine whether a student has the aptitude to go on to *lycée*.

Lycée, ages 15–18 (second, first and *terminale* years)
In the first year of *lycée* pupils choose their subjects for the *baccalauréat* (equivalent to A levels) taken in their *terminale* (final) year.

School year
The year is split into three terms, which are broken into six-week blocks by half-term breaks. The terms run from September to December with a ten-day break in late October; from January to mid-April with a break in March; and from early May to the end of June. The long summer holiday runs through July and August.

French school holidays are staggered to prevent congestion on the roads. The specific dates will vary from place to place.

The school week is Monday, Tuesday, Thursday and Friday, 8.30 to 11.30 a.m. and 1.30 to 4.30 p.m. On Wednesday and Saturday the hours are 8.30 to 11.30 a.m. Nursery and primary school children usually have Wednesdays off.

Learning the language
The French are proud of their language, and many resent the Anglicizing that's come about in recent years, with the adoption of words such as '*le weekend*'. They particularly dislike the fact that many Brits and Americans won't even try to speak French, so if you want to fit in, make learning the language a top priority.

Get Around

France is a big country with a wide variety of scenery, so make sure you get out and explore it. With excellent roads and public transport, there's really no excuse not to.

On the road

Trunk roads in France are good. The autoroutes are fast, well maintained and generally congestion-free, and can be a joy to drive on after the clogged-up British arterial routes. However, you do have to pay for them at frequent *péages* (toll booths). If you do not want to pay, use the Bison Fute map (free from petrol stations) to find alternative routes (often signed as *itineraire bis*).

Town driving, particularly in Paris, is fast, chaotic, aggressive and emotional, which perhaps explains why the accident rate in France is twice that of the UK.

Insurance

At least third-party insurance with no limit on liability is required by law in France, although fully comprehensive insurance is advisable if you can afford it. Shop around for the best deal.

Trains

France has the most extensive rail network in western Europe. The national rail service, *Société Nationale des Chemins de Fer* (SNCF), runs fast, modern trains, including *trains à grand vitesse* (TGV – very fast trains), which are often held up as the shining example of all that is right with the French railways – and all that is wrong with ours. The 300-km/h service has a line linking Calais, Paris and Lille, another linking Paris to Marseille and the Mediterranean, and a third to Bordeaux and the Spanish border.

The Paris–Marseille journey takes just three hours and can be quicker and less hassle than catching an internal flight.

A range of reductions and train passes are available from main stations and travel agents.

Driving Tips
- The French drive on the right.
- The car on the right always has the right of way unless there are lights, stop or yield signs.
- Children under ten must travel in the back.
- Seat-belts must be worn at all times.
- Rear seat-belts are compulsory.
- All French-registered cars must display a *vignette* (road tax sticker). This is bought annually in November from any *tabac* (tobacconist), and must be displayed from the first week in December. The price will vary according to your car's specifications and age.
- Your car insurance company provides you with several *constat amiables* (accident report forms). One of these and a pen should be kept in your glove compartment at all times. If you have a crash, the form needs to be filled in and signed by both parties before being forwarded to both insurance companies. The police do not get involved unless someone is injured.
- Fines for driving violations are exacted on the spot, and only cash is accepted.

Buses

Town and country bus services are good and well used. Where train lines have been closed, they have often been replaced by SNCF buses, which are free to people with a rail pass. Tickets can be bought from station ticket offices or on the bus (although it is sometimes more expensive to buy when you board). Punch your ticket in the machine provided when you get on the bus.

Internal flights

The domestic airline industry has recently been opened up to competition, which has been good for travellers and resulted in cheaper prices. Among those who operate domestic routes are Air France, Air Lib, Air Littoral Corse Méditerranée and Corsair. If you manage to get a good deal with a budget airline, flying may not be much more expensive than going by train.

Get a Life

We call them 'frogs', they sneeringly refer to us as *les rosbifs*. The rivalry between Britain and France has a long and colourful history, and the Duke of Wellington, architect of the victory at Waterloo, opined, 'We always have been, we are, and I hope that we always shall be detested in France.' If you believe the clichés, you'd think his hope had been fulfilled.

'France would be perfect if it weren't for the French' is another saying trotted out regularly. But like all clichés, the grain of truth is grossly exaggerated, and beneath their sometimes gruff exterior, many French citizens are warm, funny, witty and charming. In fact, as Peter Maslen points out, the laid-back outlook of the French is one of the things that make France such a relaxing place to live:

'People here just don't put so much pressure on themselves. I think stress is the number one problem facing most Brits – French people don't know what stress is! I feel happier and much more relaxed here and I spend much more time with my family.'

Making friends

The biggest favour you can do yourself with the locals is to try to speak their language as best you can. Persevere. Even the hardest Parisian heart will eventually warm to your efforts.

Despite the popular myth that the French refuse to speak English, many have worked hard to learn the language and relish the opportunity to use it. The exception might be in very touristy areas, where they are, understandably, less patient with foreigners' demands.

Remember that niceties matter to the French. Although they can seem rude to us, their manners are just different – it doesn't mean they are not there. Just making the effort to say '*Bonjour madame/monsieur/ mademoiselle*' when you arrive in a shop and '*Merci, au revoir*' when you leave will make a difference. And don't make the mistake of shouting '*Garçon*' in a restaurant. These days a simple '*S'il vous plaît*' is how it's done.

Expats

If you move to the countryside, the rural grapevine will spread the news, and it won't be long before local expats know about you, or the local shopkeeper tells you where other Brits are living. Remember that expats in France tend not to form ghettoes as they do in Spain and Portugal. They want to integrate into the French way of life, not just enjoy the better weather. They are also thinner on the ground and more spread out, so can be harder to bump into.

You can learn about your local community by looking at the British Embassy website (see page 154) and going to the section for the consulate that covers your region. They have a section listing Anglo societies and contacts that covers everything from cricket, churches and libraries to Scottish dancing and dining clubs.

Shopping

Many would say that shopping in France is among the best in the world. Design and quality are generally good and can come at surprisingly reasonable prices. At the other end of the scale, the range of luxury goods is superb – but if you've just relocated and are saving your euros, wait until the sales (*soldes*). Sale periods are regulated by law and take place in January and July. This is worth remembering if you need to buy expensive items, such as furniture and other household goods.

Opening hours

Most shops open Monday to Saturday from 9 or 10 a.m. to 6.30 or 7 p.m. Supermarkets and hypermarkets may stay open until 8 p.m. Sunday opening is legally limited to grocers, bakers, patisseries, florists and businesses catering only to tourists.

Markets start at 6 a.m. and finish around 1 or 1.30 p.m.

Many businesses shut down completely during August, which is the traditional holiday period.

Food

For most of us food shopping is frankly a bit of a drudge, but in France it becomes a whole new sensory experience.

Of course, there are well-stocked supermarkets and huge out-of-town hypermarkets, such as Carrefour and Leclerc, but take a lead from the French and watch how they do it at the local market. This is where you will find the best of what your area has to offer. Sampling the produce and quizzing the stall-holders can give you more insight into the culture of your region than any guidebook.

Of course, your village, town or suburb will have its own local shops, and the shopkeepers are living proof that personal service is alive and well. The availability of freshly baked bread every day has got to be one of the great joys of 'la vie en France'.

Eating out

The French love eating – and they love eating out. Over 20% of expenditure on food in France is spent in restaurants, so it is not surprising that there are places to eat to suit every taste and budget. *Prix fixe* (fixed price) menus offer especially good value. Below is a brief guide to the different types of 'eatery' you will be tempted by.

Auberges: Originally roadside inns outside towns, auberges are now usually picturesque restaurants offering dishes often typical of the region.

Bistros/Café-restaurants: Although these places can be a bit old-fashioned, they offer good, simple cooking at reasonable prices.

Brasseries: Usually located in town centres, these are cheap and cheerful bars, open all day and often throughout the night to catch people coming out of nightclubs.

Relais routiers: Found on A roads and frequented by lorry drivers, these simple restaurants offer decent food at very reasonable prices.

Restaurants: Meals served only at standard mealtimes. Prices differ tremendously, according to standards.

Restaurants rapides: Fast food outlets, offering delicious snacks such as croque monsieur, not the highly processed stuff we associate with fast food in the UK.

Tipping is not expected in restaurants, as a 15% service charge is included in the bill. If service is particularly exceptional, you can leave a tip, but it should be a matter of small change rather than the 10% we are used to in the UK.

Cinema

French cinema can be refreshingly original and unexpected after a diet of Hollywood films. Most English-language films are dubbed, but if you really can't stand hearing Arnie growl '*Je reviendrai*', then look in the listings for titles followed by VO (*version originale*) or VOST (*version originale sous-titrée*).

Staying in touch

The French postal service (*La Poste*) is efficient, but every address *must* include the five-digit postcode that follows the name of the town.

The French telephone system (*France Télécom*) was terrible until about 25 years ago, but massive investment during the 1980s and 1990s means it is now one of the most sophisticated in the world.

To telephone France from the UK dial 00 33 and omit the first zero of the French number.
To telephone the UK from France dial 00 44 and omit the first zero of the UK number.

Emergencies

France has various free numbers that you can telephone in the event of emergency.

Dial 17 for the police (*gendarmes*); 15 for an ambulance; 18 for the fire brigade (*pompiers*).

Note: The French police have the right to stop and search you at any time. If you are stopped, remain calm and be polite.

Steps to Social Success

- When you are introduced to someone for the first time, shake hands and say '*Bonjour monsieur/madame*'.
- It is usual for people who know each other to kiss on both cheeks in greeting.
- If you're invited to someone's house, always take a gift. The host will usually choose the wine to accompany the meal, so flowers, chocolates or something for the hostess would be appropriate. (If you take flowers, do not choose chrysanthemums as they are for cemeteries.)
- Cutting the 'nose' (the pointed part) of the cheese is rude.
- Splitting the bill in restaurants is not as common as it is here. Often it is the person who did the inviting who picks up the tab.
- Money and income are not polite topics of conversation.
- Personal relationships are important. Make time to get to know and socialize with people. They will be much more likely to help you when you need it.

5

Spain

There is a lot more to Spain than the Costas. Shielded (or isolated, depending on your point of view) from the rest of Europe by the Pyrenees, Spain has always been less a nation and more a union of very different and fiercely proud regions. It is geographically diverse – from cool, damp Galicia to arid Andalucia – and these differences are reflected in all aspects of the culture and character of the different regions. Try asking a Galician and an Andalucian how to make *gazpacho*, or taste *paella* in Catalonia and Murcia – they couldn't be more different. Each region puts its own individual slant on Spain's national dishes – and each, of course, is the best.

While the regions and their languages were stifled until 1975 under the fascist regime of General Franco, the current situation is very different. Since 1978, 17 regions (*autonomias*) have been created, with each having significant devolved powers. This has created a growing pride in regional language and culture, and some more militant regions, such as Catalonia, are powerful forces in national government. But the flip side of the coin is a big increase in bureaucracy.

Politics
The dictator General Franco held power in Spain from 1939 to 1975, and there were no democratic elections in the country during that period. However, within a year of his death political parties were legalized, and the first democratic elections were held in 1979. This landmark event was won by the *Union de Centro Democratica* (UCD).

Since 1975 Spain has been a constitutional monarchy, with King Juan Carlos as head of state. The left-of-centre Spanish Socialist Workers Party (*Partido Socialista Obrero Español*) was in control from 1982 to 1996. Since then, the centre-right People's Party (*Partido Popular*) has been in the ascendant, and in 2000 achieved the first absolute majority since democratic government was restored in 1975.

Parliament (*Las Cortes*) is made up of two chambers. The lower chamber, the Congress of Deputies, is elected every four years by proportional representation. The upper chamber, the Senate, has representatives elected directly by majority vote. The prime minister is the leader of the party that has most members of parliament. In August 2003, Prime Minister Jose Maria Aznar of the People's Party declared that, having spent two terms in office, he would not stand at the next election and named his deputy and spokesman, Mariano Rajoy, as his successor.

Economy

Spain is among the top ten industrialized nations in the world, but has consistently suffered the highest unemployment rate and some of the lowest wages in Europe. However, things are looking up. The government is pushing ahead with a policy of modernization and privatization, and was expecting economic growth of 3% in 2003. Alongside this, the unemployment rate has fallen from nearly 23% in 1996 to 12% in 2003. Since joining the EU in 1986, Spain, particularly the south, has done well out of subsidies.

Currency

In January 2002 the peseta was replaced by the euro.

Religion

Although there is no official religion in Spain, Catholicism is deeply ingrained in Spanish life. The country's most famous buildings, works of art and fiestas all have their roots or inspiration in Catholicism. Nearly half of Spanish school children go to Catholic schools, and 85% of Spaniards call themselves Catholic. However, church attendance is in decline, and churches far outnumber priests. Despite this, there is little doubt that the saying 'Here in Spain we are all Catholics, even the atheists' still holds true.

Time difference

Spain is on Central European Time, which is one hour ahead of GMT. Daylight Saving Time, from the last Sunday in March to the last Sunday in October, is two hours ahead of GMT (one hour ahead of British Summer Time).

Climate

Spain's weather is very varied, depending on the region you are in. During the summer, the arid central area around Madrid swelters in 'frying pan' conditions, while the mountains of the Sierra Nevada and Pyrenees are topped with snow; Galicia is warm and wet, and the Mediterranean coasts bask in relentless sunshine. The majority of winters in Spain are mild.

Brits in Spain

Spain is one of the most popular destinations for emigrating Brits, and an estimated 500,000 now count Spain as home. The largest expat communities are on the Mediterranean coasts: Alicante and the Costa Brava have some 145,000 Brits, while Malaga and the Costa del Sol have 280,000 plus. By comparison, Spain's major cities, Madrid and Barcelona, each have around 15,000.

In rural areas Brits tend to be well integrated into the Spanish community, making an active contribution to everyday life. In coastal areas, however, especially the Costas, some Brits have a tendency to create their own little slice of Britain, socializing only with Brits and not going much further than the 'geniune English pub' and the fish and chip shop. Needless to say, this can hamper any attempts to learn the language and restrict the experiences that are open to them in Spain.

Get There

The good news for British citizens – as members of the EU – is that there are no barriers to living or working in Spain. No visa is required, and getting residency is pretty much a foregone conclusion – but that doesn't mean you can rest on your laurels and pour yourself another *sangria*.

Spain is famous for its unwieldy bureaucracy, so be prepared to queue, feel frustrated and get impatient. Jill and Barrie Burgess, who relocated to Spain with their children, Billy and Nancy, during series one of *Get a New Life*, can't stress enough how important it is to be ready to face these hurdles:

'The slower pace of life really takes some adjusting to. Although you don't see people walking about with sad dreary faces, and people are more pleasant, happy and laid-back than they are in the UK, there is a downside to living in Spain. Everything takes forever. You need to think very long and very hard about making the move. The paperwork and the bureaucracy can really get you down. You've got to accept that things happen differently here.'

The alternative to dealing with all the bureaucracy yourself is to get a *gestor* – not a lawyer, but someone who makes a living from dealing with other people's forms and knows the system inside out. They can be worth their weight in gold.

To ease your arrival, here are the essentials you will need to set in motion before you go or as soon as you arrive.

Getting your residence card

As of 1 March 2003, anyone who is employed, self-employed, a student or an EU national dependent on an EU or Spanish national is no longer obliged to apply for a residence card (*residencia*). You are entitled to live in Spain so long as you have a valid passport.

Legally, pensioners and people of independent means still have to apply for a residence card within 30 days of deciding Spain is to be their country of residence. In practice, as an EU citizen, you can stay as a tourist for three months before needing to

apply. If you fall into either of these groups, or are opting to apply anyway, you will have to produce certain paperwork.

You will need...
- Passport and multiple photocopies of it
- Medical certificate (ask your GP) or private health insurance
- Evidence of income or capital, e.g. certificate available from your bank
- Marriage certificate (where applicable) and photocopies of it
- Four passport photos

The usual process takes three trips to the Foreign Nationals Office (*Oficina Gubernativa de Extranjeros*) or the national police station (*comisaría de policial*) in the province where you live. (Note that there are four different types of police station; see page 87 for details, or log on to the website of the Ministry of the Interior, details on page 155.) It then takes up to six weeks for the card to be ready, but it is not unknown for people to wait over six months.

EU nationals planning to stay indefinitely will receive a five-year residence card, known as a *tarjeta comunitaria europea* or *tarjeta de residente comunitario*). Non-EU nationals are issued with a residence card initially valid for two years, or for the duration of their work contract. Subsequent renewals are valid for five years. All foreigners who have held a normal residence permit for six years can apply for a permanent residence card.

Cards for dependents are issued for the same period granted to the principal applicant. Children under 18 may be included on a parent's permit.

Note: You can apply for a residence permit at the Spanish Embassy in the UK (see page 155). This might be advisable if your Spanish isn't up to much.

Foreigner's identification number

You will need a *número de identificación de extranjero* (NIE) for financial matters, such as opening a bank account and getting a mortgage. Apply for your NIE at your local *comisaría de policial*. You can also get the necessary forms from a Spanish lawyer. It can take up to three months to get your NIE, so it is important to apply for it as soon as you arrive.

Citizenship

You are automatically entitled to Spanish citizenship if you were born in Spain and one of your parents is Spanish, or if you were born in Spain to parents with no nationality. You can also apply for Spanish citizenship if you have had a residence permit for 10 years.

Dual nationality does not exist in Spain: the government requires you to renounce your former nationality. However, the British government doesn't accept this, so citizenship is a contentious area and expert legal advice is recommended.

Pets

There are no restrictions on taking pets into Spain from other EU countries, and no mandatory quarantine period. However, there are specific rules for different types of pets. Speak to your vet in the UK, or contact the local Spanish Consulate. See the general advice about pets in the EU section (page 36) and note Spain's general rules below:

- A certificate from your vet in the UK (with Spanish translation) must state:

Love/Hate

'The weather! It affects every aspect of life – the food you eat, the amount of exercise you do, the way you socialize – I can't remember the last time we had the heating on.'

'In my experience, INSALUD [the Spanish health service] is streets ahead of the NHS.'

'Community and family do actually still matter here. When my 83-year-old friend hadn't been seen in the local shop for a couple of days, the shopkeeper called round to check she was OK.'

'Cheaper cars, cheaper food, cheaper property, cheaper everything…'

'If you're wanting a taste of home, you can get just about everything – tea-bags, Marmite, Hobnobs – at the British-run shops.'

'Bureaucracy – it's no joke. You have to be very, very patient and prepared to queue. Losing your rag doesn't help, so take a good book.'

'The way they treat animals can be upsetting. There are huge numbers of strays in a terrible state.'

'The sense of humour is a problem. Not that it's bad – just different. More Benny Hill and lacking in irony.'

'It can be hard to meet people. Sometimes you feel like an inconvenience. If you don't speak the language, they can treat you with the same indifference they do tourists.'

'The laid-back attitude is great when you're on holiday, but can be frustrating when you're trying to do business or get things done.'

- That the pet has been in your care for at least three months
- That the pet is not intended for trade
- That the pet will be taken to a certified vet if required by legislation
• All animals must be accompanied by, or picked up by, their owner or the owner's representative.

On arrival in Spain, contact a local vet to find out if your animal needs to be registered and microchipped (mandatory for dogs). Also ask if there are any local diseases that might make extra vaccinations advisable.

Your car

If you want to take your car to Spain, there are no major obstacles. Your EU or British driving licence qualifies you to drive there, but you must register it with the traffic department (*Jefatura Provincial de Tráfico*) within six months of arrival.

As soon as your residence permit comes through, you should officially import your car, i.e. get Spanish plates. Although many expats don't bother, it can be a useful thing to do. (You have to register for Spanish plates anyway after six months, and pay a percentage tax on the car's value.) Vehicles not officially imported can, theoretically, be impounded, and insurance is more expensive on foreign-registered cars. You can arrange the importation yourself with the traffic department, but it's wise to employ specialist help with this procedure. Ask around the local expat community for recommendations.

Before you leave for Spain, make sure you have prepared your car as recommended in the EU section (see pages 36–7) and that you have a Certificate of Permanent Export (V561) from the DVLA (see page 154). You need this form regardless of whether or not you officially import your car to Spain.

Note: When driving in Spain you are legally required to carry a spare set of bulbs, spare tyres and the tools needed to change them, as well as two warning triangles (bearing the symbol E9 and code 27R03).

Other belongings

There are no customs formalities to be completed when moving your household goods within the EU. The only paperwork required is a detailed inventory that includes receipts or approximate values (in euros) for each item, which can be compiled by you or your removal firm.

If you are not going to be present at customs, your representative, i.e. the removal company, may need a photocopy of your passport, so give them one just in case.

The electricity supply in Spain is 220 volts AC with a frequency of 50 hertz (cycles). A few areas still have a 110-volt supply. Modern electrical appliances are being rationalized at 230 volts, so unless your white goods are several years old, most should be fine for use in Spain.

All but old televisions will work after slight adjustments by a TV engineer; ask around the local expat community. Spain (like the UK and most other European countries) uses the PAL–BG standard.

Get a Home

In 1991 there were 353,367 foreign nationals residing in Spain. Ten years on there were officially 1,572,017. No wonder Spanish property prices have risen astronomically – on a par with the housing boom experienced in the UK over the last decade. Within Spain, the areas of Madrid, Murcia, Andalucia and Castilla-La Mancha have seen the fastest rises. Finding a home is complicated enough in your mother tongue, so even if you do speak fluent Spanish, we would recommend making use of a professional intermediary. There are numerous estate agents who specialize in selling Spanish property to Brits. They have made it their job to know every in and out of the Spanish property system, and many have excellent websites with all the information you could possibly need. It makes sense to use their expertise. They can also recommend a good lawyer. (As in the UK, it is usual for buyer and seller to have different lawyers.)

Before you go
- Decide if you want somewhere to rent or buy
- Do some hunting on the Internet
- Make a few reconnaisance trips
- Approach an international estate agent or relocation agent
- Get multiple copies of your passport
- If you already have accommodation sorted out, make sure you know what is supplied with the property and pack accordingly.

When you arrive
- Find an English-speaking lawyer
- Start looking at the newspaper property sections (*Inmobiliaria* or *Pisos y apartementos*) and websites
- Get property details from local estate agents (*inmobiliaria*).

Renting
Most people opt to rent until they know their move is permanent and they have acquired enough local knowledge to know where they really want to live. Remember, the place that is perfect for summer holidays may not be so delightful when all the shops and restaurants shut up for winter.

Rental property, from bedsits to luxury villas and rural *fincas*, is plentiful in most of Spain, except in major cities, such as Madrid and Barcelona, where rent is high and finding what you want can be tricky and time-consuming. Rentals can also be difficult to find elsewhere during the busy holiday season of April to September.

Rental contracts and fees
- A rental contract is usually for 11 months or one year.
- The tenant has the right to renew a one-year contract for up to five years. This does not apply to an 11-month contract.
- After the first year, the tenant must give two months' notice (one month, if leaving the country).
- The first month's rent is payable after signing the contract.
- A returnable deposit of one month's rent is required for unfurnished property, and two months' rent for furnished.
- The monthly rent is increased annually by the figure published in the National Consumer Trade Index. The tenant must be informed about the increase in writing by the owner at least one month before it is applied.
- The estate agent's fee will be either one month's rent, or 10% of one year's rent, plus VAT at 16%. There may also be some small administration and registration fees.

Repairs and maintenance
The owner must leave the property clean and in perfect condition, with everything in working order. For the first 30 days of your lease the owner takes responsibility for breakages and malfunctions, and must sort out repairs. After this period, the owner remains responsible for any major or structural repairs, such as a leaking roof, but the tenant becomes responsible for fixing any damage

that results from everyday wear and tear, such as a broken window blind or a leaking tap. However, most good landlords will carry out all repairs and keep the property in good order if the tenant lets them know what needs doing.

Unfurnished Property

While accommodation in popular holiday areas is often furnished down to the last teaspoon, rental property in both cities and rural areas is usually unfurnished in the most literal sense: no light fittings, no bulbs, no curtain rails… Arriving with these items – and a toolkit – is therefore a wise precaution.

Unfurnished can also mean there are no carpets or kitchen fittings, but there is usually bathroom porcelain. If this is the case with the property you choose to rent, you might be able to buy fixtures from the previous tenant. If that's not possible and the place is a shell, it might be worth asking the landlord to fit the items for you if you pay. Whatever you decide, make sure you know exactly what is in the accommodation before you sign.

Property tax

The main local property tax in Spain is called *Impuesto de Bienes Inmuebles* (IBI). This is very similar to British council tax and is payable annually to the town hall. The amount charged is a percentage based on how much the property is worth, and varies from place to place. As a tenant, you pay IBI to the owner of the property, usually with the annual increase in rent. It is then the responsibility of the owner to pay tax on the property.

Insurance

The tenant is nearly always responsible for contents insurance. The owner will normally have buildings insurance, but is under no legal obligation to do so. The situation should be made clear in the lease. If he has no insurance, it is up to you as the tenant to make sure the property is covered.

Community charges

If you're renting an apartment, or a town-house with a communal garden and pool, the rent should include the community charges, which cover expenses such as wages for the *conserje* (caretaker), the upkeep of pool and garden, and the cleaning of communal areas. However, this can be charged on top of the rent, so check the contract before signing.

Learning the rules

Establishing yourself as part of any new community can be difficult, so here are some tips to ease your path.

- Each community has its own peculiar rules, which can change from year to year, so make sure you know what they are.
- Community rules for rented apartments usually do not allow you to barbecue on your terrace, unless there is a proper built-in barbecue, with a chimney for the smoke.
- Domestic animals generally cannot be exercised in the communal garden.
- There is often a limit as to the number of guests you can invite to use the communal facilities, such as swimming pools and tennis courts.

Buying

Although buying in Spain is no more difficult than buying in the UK, it is different, so always employ a Spanish property lawyer from the outset. Your local consulate in Spain can give you a list of English-speaking lawyers.

One of the main pitfalls to be aware of is that if there are any unpaid bills or mortgages on a property when you buy, the seller's creditors can exercise their right to take the property even after you have paid for it. For this reason it is essential that the Land Registry (*Registro de Propiedad*) is thoroughly searched by your lawyer before the sale goes through. The registry will confirm the description of the property, its boundaries and reveal any outstanding mortgages. The British Embassy in Spain recommends getting your lawyer to confirm in writing that there are no mortgages or other debts on the property to ensure that the registry has been properly checked.

It is also wise to consider getting all legal documents translated into English by a trusted third party so that you know exactly what you are signing. It may seem like an added cost now but it could save you from disaster later.

For further advice about buying property in Spain, contact the Foundation Institute of Foreign Property Owners (see page 155). In general, the process has five steps.

1. Reservation agreement

Having decided on a property, your first move is to pay a small deposit of €500–€1200 (or 1–2% of the purchasing price). The property should then be withdrawn from the market while your lawyer makes the initial *Nota Simple* (Land Registry) checks. This usually takes four or five days.

2. Private contract of purchase and sale

Within a week or two a private agreement is signed between the parties, and at this stage you pay 10% of the agreed price directly to the vendor. Your lawyers should by now have thoroughly checked the deeds of the building and all outstanding debts and rates, such as IBI, community fees, electricity and water bills, which are taken into account in the private contract.

3. Bank bond or insurance certificate

If the property is still being built, the developer is legally bound to provide the buyer with a bank bond or insurance certificate as a guarantee against debts incurred during construction. This protects the buyer if, for some reason, the property is not finished. In that case, the bank or insurance company will refund the money paid by the buyer plus 6% interest. Some builders flout the law and don't have this bond or insurance, so do check before parting with a deposit.

4. Title deed

It is very important for your lawyer to check that the title deed (*escritura de compraventa*) is in order. It should include the freehold of the apartment and the freehold to a fixed percentage of the communal areas, such as staircase, gardens and swimming pool. This determines the owner's contribution to the general maintenance of the property.

5. Completion

This takes place in front of a public notary (*notario*), who is solely concerned that the legal requirements have been met. He issues the title deed. If the purchase is financed with a mortgage, the bank representatives are present in order to pay and sign the mortgage. Your title to the property becomes final when the details are entered in the Land Registry. This should be done as soon as possible after the *escritura* is signed. The British Embassy recommends that you ask your lawyer for a Land Registry certificate to prove this has been done.

Additional costs

You should allow an extra 7.5–10% of the advertised price to complete a property purchase, and up to 20% if purchasing a plot of land. This covers:

- Municipal tax – usually paid by the vendor, but not always
- Lawyer's fees – usually 1% of the purchase price plus VAT
- Notary and Land Registry fees – average €900–€1200, depending on the price of the property
- VAT and Stamp Duty – 7% VAT plus 1% Stamp Duty on new homes; 7% Stamp Duty and no VAT on second-hand homes; 16% VAT plus 1% Stamp Duty on villa plots
- You will need to add an extra 2% to your costs if mortgaging with a Spanish bank.

Mortgages

Spanish mortgage lenders (*hipotecas*) are generally regarded as very competitive. There is the usual range of banks and high street lenders, so shop around to make sure you get the best deal. Main lenders include Banco Vizcaya-Bilbao and Banco de Santander.

In Spain most mortgage lenders automatically hold your home as security, and the lender's charge over the property is recorded at the land registry

Lots of Spanish banks try to insist that you take their home insurance as part of a mortgage package. You are not legally obliged to do this, so don't be talked into it before you've looked into other insurance deals.

What mortgage can I get as a percentage of property value?

The norm is 60–70% of bank valuation of the property, regardless of purchase price. It is important to fully consider all additional costs before you leave the UK.

Jill and Barrie Burgess certainly found buying in Spain more costly than they had first thought:

'Buying a property here is far more expensive and difficult than we ever imagined. With the money we had to spend, we thought we would be able to buy two houses – one to live in and one to rent out. In the end we could only afford one, and even then it is much smaller than we had hoped for.

'Also, there seems to have been a trend in Spain for building houses on any old bit of land to make a fast buck out of the English. Many of these houses have no planning permission whatsoever. We ended up buying the fifth house we went for – we had started the conveyance procedure with four others, only to find they were totally illegal. The authorities are trying to clamp down, but buying a house here is still a legal and financial minefield.'

What mortgage can I get as a percentage of my income?

Your monthly mortgage repayment should be no more than one-third of your income after tax and other liabilities, such as debt repayments. Your calculated income will include worldwide sources, but ignores any projected rental income from Spanish property.

What if I'm unemployed?

It is unlikely you will get a mortgage unless you can prove you have a regular income.

Are there any charges?

All banks charge a set-up fee of 1–2% of the lending required; this will be deducted from your deposit. On top of the set-up fee you must pay 1% on the loan for Stamp Duty, plus notary and Treasury fees.

Note: The loan will be in euros, so if your income is in sterling, don't forget to take

exchange rate fluctuations into account before deciding to go for a Spanish mortgage.

How long will it take?

Decisions on mortgage approval take much the same amount of time as in the UK. It really does depend on the lender, so always make sure you get an estimated deadline for a response when you apply.

How is interest calculated?

The *Euribor* (official rate) is published monthly. Your rate is determined by the *Euribor* in the month you complete. A competitive rate would be around *Euribor* plus 1–1.25%.

Your interest rate is usually re-calculated once a year, and gives you a fixed rate for the next 12 months.

How long have I got to pay back the loan?

Terms range from five to 25 years, but most lenders will look for the mortgage to be paid up by the time you are aged 70.

What if I want to pay it off early?

Most banks, but not all, run redemption penalties for the lifetime of the loan. These, on average, are 1% of the amount redeemed.

Connecting utilities

Electricity is supplied by several regional companies in Spain. To get connected, find their number in the local phone book. They tend to send out bills every two months.

Mains gas is also supplied by local companies, who are listed in the local phone book. Bills are sent out every two months. In most areas of Spain, gas bottles (*bombonas*) are delivered by Repsol Butano. You need to contact the local agent to arrange a contract for supply and delivery.

Water supply is a local matter in Spain, controlled either by the municipality or a private company. In most areas there is a standing quarterly charge or a monthly charge for a minimum consumption (*canón de consumo*). As Spain is a dry, sometimes arid, country, water can rapidly become a scarce resource, so use it with care.

Compañia Telefónica Nacional de España (CNTE), usually known just as Telefónica, is the Spanish telephone service. To get a phone installed, reconnected, or to change the name on an account you must visit Telefónica's local office.

You will need...
- Passport or residence permit
- A copy of your property deed (*escritura*) or rental contract

Note: A deposit of around €200 is payable if you rent rather than own your home and don't have a residence permit

Telephone bills are sent out monthly, and there are three tariffs for domestic calls. The peak rate is Monday to Friday, 8 a.m. to 5 p.m., and Saturday, 8 a.m. to 2 p.m. The normal rate is Monday to Friday, 5 to 10 p.m. The reduced rate (30% cheaper than peak time) is Monday to Friday, 10 p.m. to 8 a.m., Saturday, 2 p.m. to midnight, and all day on Sundays and public holidays.

It's advisable to pay utility bills by direct debit (*transferencia*) from a Spanish bank account. In fact, some companies insist on this.

TV licence
You do not need a television licence in Spain.

Get a Job

Spain is governed by the EU directives outlined in the introduction to this section. As an EU citizen, you have the right to work in Spain but, as it has one of the highest unemployment rates in Europe, don't count on walking into a job. Tourism, property, insurance and finance offer most opportunities for expats. There are also labour shortages in agriculture and construction.

Although the working day is still punctuated by a siesta, the habit is becoming less common as foreign companies move in with different working practices. However, socializing and having long lunches with colleagues and customers remain essential parts of the business culture.

Before you go
- Unless you aim to work in the tourist industry, learning the language is essential. Start before you leave the UK.
- Look in the employment sections of British newspapers or the *International Herald Tribune* (see page 154).
- Look up the European Employment Services (EURES) database (see page 154) and ask the advisers at your local job centre.
- Get a list of British companies operating in Spain from the British Embassy.
- Validating your UK qualifications for use in Spain can be a long, complex process. Some are covered by EU agreements, other aren't (see page 154)
- Prepare a CV and keep it brief (two pages maximum).

Once you arrive
- You do not need a residence card to start looking for work, so keep looking in British newspapers and start looking in the local press at the jobs section (*sección empleo*).
- You can also place your own advert in the 'situations wanted' (*demanda*) section of many papers.

- Contact your local Chamber of Commerce (*Cámara Oficial de Comercio*) for lists of companies in your area.
- Visit the local office of the National Employment Institute (*Instituto Naciónal de Empleo*). The INEM can prove crucial to your chances of success as it is the only agency allowed to deal with recruitment for permanent jobs.
- Private Spanish employment agencies, which tend to be concentrated in big cities, can recruit only for temporary positions.
- Most big cities have international employment agencies recruiting for Spanish employers. Look for details in the phone book.

Applying for jobs

Spain is notorious for the amount of time it takes to do anything, so it can be weeks or even months between applying for a job and starting work. Don't expect anything to happen fast: nothing does.

Word of mouth has a powerful influence in Spain, so make as many contacts as possible among both locals and expats, and keep your ear to the ground. Many employers take on up to 50% of their staff through personal recommendation.

Employment contracts

When you're offered a job, you will get an employment contract (*contrato de trabajo*). There are two main contract types: permanent or temporary, the latter usually for a year. You can be employed for three consecutive years under one-year contracts. After that your employer must either hire you permanently or let you go.

Your contract will be made out in Spanish and include details such as pay, working hours, term of employment, duties and any benefits.

The working week is officially 37 ½ hours. You can't be forced to work overtime in Spain, and you're not allowed to work more than 80 hours' overtime in any one year. Overtime must be paid at least 75% over your normal hourly rate.

The average annual holiday (excluding the ten national holidays) is at least four weeks.

The average monthly wage is €1600, and the minimum wage (*salario minimo*) is €15.04 per day or €451 per month.

If you want to set up your own business or be self-employed, the British Consulate website (see page 155) has information about forms you might need for different professions.

Further information about all aspects of working in Spain is available from the Labour Office of the Spanish Embassy in London (*Oficina Labora*), see page 155.

Get Healthy

Like the NHS, Spain's state health service (INSALUD) is great in emergencies, but suffers problems with bed shortages and waiting lists. Similarly, the quality of care and waiting time varies from place to place.

As an EU citizen with a form E111, you are entitled to the same state services and benefits as any native Spaniard for a limited period and with minimum fuss before you need to get into the system. Contact the Spanish Embassy (see page 155) for more details about the preliminary period of cover.

INSALUD covers:
- GP and specialist consultations
- Hospitalization
- Tests
- Discounted drugs and medicines
- Basic dental care
- Ante- and post-natal care

- Ambulance services
- Appliances (e.g. wheelchairs)

INSULAD contributions are taken out of your earnings at source. While the national health system is adequate, completely free treatment is available only in certain hospitals, where waiting lists can be very long. Many people therefore choose to take out private cover so that they can get treatment more quickly.

Getting into the Spanish health system

Although reciprocal EU agreements mean that you will probably not have to register with *Seguridad Social* (Social Security) for two years, you will have to do so to get the full benefits of the Spanish health system. Here's how.

Before you leave the UK

If you are not going straight into a job, get social security form E106 from the Post Office. (Pensioners and those on invalidity benefit need form E121.)

If you *are* going into a job, your employer will usually deal with the formalities of registering you with social security.

On arrival

Take the appropriate E form plus the documents listed below to the local office of the *Instituto Nacional de la Seguridad Social* (INSS), which you can find in the *Yellow Pages* under '*Seguridad Social*' or from your local town hall (*casa consistorial*).

You will need…

- Passports and (certified) birth certificates for you and all dependents
- Marriage certificate (if applicable)
- Proof of residence, such as a property deed of sale (escritura) or a rental contract

Four to eight weeks later you will get…

- Social security card (*cartilla de seguridad social* or *tarjeta sanitaria*)
- List of local medical practitioners and hospitals
- General information about services and charges

Married couples with one partner working are covered by the same social security card and number, as are all dependents (e.g. children under 16) who are listed on your social security card.

Further information about social security can be obtained from *Instituto Nacional de la Seguridad Social* (see page 155).

When you get your social security card you will be assigned a local GP (*médico de cabecera*), or you can just register with the nearest one. You may be able to switch GPs, depending on availability.

No payment is made when visiting a public health service doctor. Just show your social security card or E111 form.

Private health insurance

In some cases, social security covers 75% of treatment; the other 25% must be paid by the patient or a supplementary insurance scheme. Most people who can afford it take out private health insurance, which offers a wider choice and gets around the waiting lists.

Hospitals

A list of local hospitals and health centres treating social security patients is available from your local social security office. If you're covered by INSALUD, you must show your social security card. If not, you need your E111 or evidence of your health insurance or the ability to pay. Documentation is not needed up front to get emergency treatment.

Pharmacies

Indicated by a green or red cross, pharmacies are open Monday to Saturday, 9.30 a.m. to 1.30 p.m. and 4.30 to 8.00 p.m. Details of the nearest 24-hour pharmacy (*farmacia de guardia*) will be displayed on the door.

Pharmacies have a monopoly on non-prescription drugs in Spain, which means you can't buy them anywhere else.

You will have to pay 40% of prescription costs, unless you are retired or have a disability, in which case prescriptions are free.

Get Wealthy

This section fills you in on handling your finances in Spain, covering everything from banks and bills to taxes and wills.

Banks

There are two types of bank in Spain: retail banks (*bancos*) and savings banks (*cajas de ahorros*).

Retail banks are clearing banks, and those with the largest networks are Banco Santander, Banco Atlantico, Banco Banesto, Banco Central Hispano, Banco Bilbao Vizcaya (BBV), Banco Popular and Argentaria.

Savings banks offer a more personal service than the clearing banks. They provide the same basic services but aren't recommended for international business. The three largest savings banks are La Caixa, Caja de Madrid and Caja Postal.

Opening a bank account

To open a current account (*cuenta de ahorro con talonario* or *cuenta corriente*) you will need

a residence permit. If you haven't yet got your permit, you can open a non-resident's account (*cuenta de no-residente*).

Once your residence permit has been granted, you must advise your bank, who will then change your account to a resident's account (*cuenta de residente*).

You will need…
- Passport
- Residence permit
- Proof of your address in Spain
- Your foreigner's identification number (NIE)

Non-residents need to produce just their passport and a certificate of non-residence. Many banks will apply for this on behalf of the client, and charge a small commission. Others ask the client to provide the certificate. Alternatively, you may just be asked to sign a statement saying you will pay UK tax on any interest.

Cheques
Banks do not issue cheque guarantee cards, so most shops do not accept cheques. As a result, the Spanish tend to prefer cash, cards and direct debit for everyday transactions.

Cheques are paid on presentation, as long as there are enough funds to cover them. If you do write a cheque, you must write the date in words, not figures.

Withdrawing cash
Your bank will give you a cashpoint/debit card. As in the UK, you can take out money at any machine, but may be charged if you use the machine of a bank with which you do not have an account.

Bank charges
Spanish banks have some of the highest charges in Europe for day-to-day

transactions, such as writing cheques, executing standing orders and direct debits, and handling credit card transactions. Get a list of charges before opening an account and compare them with those of other banks.

Bank statements
Statements (*extracto* or *avance*) are sent monthly or quarterly, although you can request one at any time just by asking.

Banking hours
Although hours vary, banks are generally open Monday to Friday from 8.30 or 9 a.m. to 2.00 p.m.

Taxes
All residents of Spain, including foreigners, are subject to personal taxation on their worldwide income. Non-residents are subject to taxation on income from Spanish sources. In other words, if you have property in Spain but reside in another country, income earned from that property would be liable to Spanish taxation.

Residence for tax purposes is defined as anyone living in Spain for 183 days or over in any one calendar year. If you are resident in Spain for more than 183 days in any year, the Spanish authorities will tax you on the income you may have earned (and been taxed on) in another country.

The tax liability of expatriates transferring to Spain is often confusing, so make sure you take professional advice. It is possible to be resident in two countries simultaneously for tax purposes, or, alternatively, to spend a year without being resident in any country at all.

The tax year in Spain runs from 1 January to 31 December. Most taxes are based on self-assessment, so you report and calculate your own tax – or face penalties. Tax forms must be bought by taxpayers from a tobacconist's (*estanco*), but some are available only from a tax office (*agencia tributaria*). You must lodge an annual income tax declaration between 1 May and 20 June, or by 30 June if applying for a refund. The majority of Spaniards seek expert help with their tax declarations, so it is especially advisable to seek help if Spanish isn't your native tongue.

If you are working, you will be taxed at source – effectively, a payment in advance. Once you have calculated your tax liability, take away the payment already made and this is the tax you owe. If you have overpaid, you receive a refund.

Here are some of the main taxes likely to affect you:

Income tax (*Impuesto sobre la renta de las personas físicas*)

IRPF is payable on worldwide income. Thanks to a large number of deductions, Spanish income tax rates are among the lowest in Europe, but rates for high-income individuals top 50%.

Value added tax (*Impuesto sobre el valor anadido*)

IVA, which Brits know as VAT, is included in the price of most goods in shops. There are three rates of IVA in Spain: 4% on staple foods, such as bread and fruit, and newspapers; 7% on other foodstuffs, fuel and medication; 16% on other goods and services, including utility bills.

Wealth tax (*Impuesto sobre el patrimonio*)

If you are resident in Spain, you must calculate the value of all your assets, including property, motor vehicles, business assets, cash in bank accounts, stocks and shares and jewellery. For residents there is a tax-free allowance of around €150,000 for a principle residence, plus €108,000 for other assets. There is no allowance for non-residents, who must pay wealth tax on Spanish assets, usually a property. Assets are taxed progressively from 0.2% to 2.5%.

As with all areas of tax, this is enormously complicated, and it pays to take legal advice.

Inheritance and gift tax (*Impuesto sobre sucesiones y donaciones*)

Payable on worldwide assets, this tax can be very expensive. Check your position with an accountant.

Property or real estate tax (*Impuesto sobre bienes inmuebles urbano*)

Like UK council tax, the Spanish property tax is paid annually and goes towards local services. It is generally calculated at around 0.3% of the rateable value of rural properties, and around 0.5% of the rateable value in towns and cities. Some authorities, however, charge as much as 2%. Rateable value is somewhere around three-quarters of market value.

When you buy a home in Spain, register the purchase with the town hall within two months or you could be fined for non-payment of tax.

Capital gains tax (*Impuesto sobre incremento de patrimonio de la venta de un bien inmueble*)

A tax is payable on the profits made on the sale of property and other assets located in Spain. This is a very complicated area of taxation beyond the scope of this book, so you must seek expert advice.

Business tax (*Impuesto sobre actividades económicas*)

IAE, as this is now known (it was formerly called *licencia fiscal*), is paid once a year by all businesses, including the self-employed.

Company or corporation tax (*Impuesto sobre sociedades*)

Profits by partnerships and registered companies, such as a *Sociedad Anónima* (SA) or *Sociedad Limitada* (SL), are subject to this tax at 35%.

Pensions

Whether you are employed or self-employed, your social security contributions go towards a state pension. Few companies in Spain have their own pension scheme.

As in the UK, a state pension may turn out to be too little to live on, so it is wise to pay into a private pension fund.

Wills

Inheritance is an area where you must take legal *and* financial advice or you might end up paying taxes on your entire estate in both Spain and the UK. However, with sensible planning, both UK inheritance tax and Spanish succession tax can be minimized. For example, UK expats should have at least two wills: one for the assets in Spain and another in the UK covering assets located outside Spain. It is also important to recognize that, apart from the need for suitable wills, you will need to observe the law regarding succession (see below).

Remember…

- In Spain a spouse is not a 'protected' beneficiary. Under Spanish succession law, your children have a prior right to benefit from your estate before your spouse.
- If you make a Spanish will and subsequently change your English will, make sure your English solicitor knows about the Spanish will. English wills include a provision that automatically revokes all earlier wills, and if there is

no reference to the Spanish will, you could inadvertently revoke it.

Get Wise

Education in Spain is compulsory from ages six to sixteen and free from pre-school to eighteen. However, expect to pay for school books, stationery and extra-curricular activities, such as sports and arts and crafts.

If you have a preference for a particular school, it's important to buy or rent a home within that school's catchment area. Villages and suburbs have their own nursery and primary schools, but secondary schools have larger catchment areas and may necessitate a longer journey.

The only schools in Spain that teach exclusively in English are foreign and international private schools. Multilingual international schools teach pupils in both English and Spanish.

The British Council (see page 155) can supply lists of English schools in Spain; most are members of the National Association of British Schools.

To enrol your children in a primary or secondary Spanish school, go to the town hall or Ministry of Education (*Ministerio de Education*) and get a list of schools in your area. You might need to produce your children's birth certificates or passports, and their school records. (Get a copy of the latter, with a translation, before you leave the UK.) Sometimes the school records are unnecessary because Spanish schools assess children in their first year and hold them back or put them up a year if they think it appropriate. Note that some schools insist on interviewing children and setting them an exam before enrolment.

Spain's education system

Here's a quick rundown of what you can expect to encounter when you dip a toe into Spain's education system.

Pre-school, ages 1–6 (*Preescuelar*)

This is voluntary and includes nursery school (*guardería*), kindergarten (*jardín de la infancia*) and infant school (*escuela infantil*). Pre-school is divided into two parts: cycle one (*Ciclo 1º*) for ages one to three and cycle two (*Ciclo 2º*) for ages four to six.

Nursery school is highly recommended, particularly if your children are going to continue with a state education. After one or two years of nursery school they will be integrated into the local community and will have learnt Spanish in preparation for primary school.

As pre-school is not compulsory, you are not guaranteed a place at a state nursery. However, private nurseries are inexpensive and good value.

Compulsory education, ages 6–14 (*Escolaridad obligatoria*)

On completing what is known as basic general education (*educación general básica* or EGB), pupils receive a school-leaving certificate, which determines the course of their future education (see below).

Technical school, ages 14–16 (*Formación profesional*)

Less academically gifted pupils are awarded a *certificado de escolaridad* at the end of their EGB, and attend a vocational school. The first (compulsory) year covers general career teaching. The second (optional) year allows students to specialize in a subject of their course, and includes work placements. Students who successfully complete both years gain a certificate.

High school, ages 14–18 (*Instituto de educación secundaria*)

Those obtaining high marks at the end of their EGB are awarded a *título de graduado escolar* certificate and attend an academic secondary school to study for their baccalaureate (*bachillerato*).

School year

The year runs from the first week in September to the middle or end of June and is made up of three terms, each averaging around 11 weeks.

The hours vary from school to school, but are usually 9 a.m. to 4 p.m. with a one-hour break for lunch. However, increasing numbers of schools don't have a lunch break, and instead finish the day early at 2 p.m.

Spanish schoolchildren have long school holidays compared with those in many other countries. The main ones are at Christmas, Easter and during the summer. Dates are published locally well in advance, allowing parents plenty of time to schedule family holidays.

Learning the language

If you don't speak Spanish, you should start learning straight away. In business, English is increasingly understood and spoken, but the average man on the street does not speak English, unless you are in a popular tourist area. So if you intend working in Spain, you will have little choice but to learn Spanish; in fact, you will severely limit your job options if you do not.

Formal language qualifications for non-native speakers of Spanish (*diplomas de Español como lengua extranjera*) are administered by the Spanish Ministry of Education, the *Instituto Cervantes* and the University of Salamanca. Information is available from the above institutions or Spanish embassies, and examinations are held worldwide at three levels (beginner, intermediate and advanced).

Castillian Spanish is spoken in Madrid and is the official language, but the regionality referred to earlier has led to a growing use of 'minority' languages, particularly Catalan, Basque, Galician and Valencian. If you live in a region that speaks one of these languages, it can be useful to learn a few words so that you can at least make out signs and menus.

Get Around

As in most other countries, city roads are usually well maintained and public transport is generally very efficient, but this is not always true of rural parts of Spain, so be prepared for mixed conditions.

On the road

There are no grey areas when driving in Spain: rural roads are picturesque and empty, while city roads are noisy, overcrowded nightmares. The one surprise is that Spanish motorways are also deserted – the result of their private owners charging high tolls.

Petrol is traditionally reasonably priced, so driving is probably the best option for long journeys if you're watching the pennies.

On the whole Spanish drivers do tend to be (dare we say it?) a bit scary, so drive with caution.

Insurance

Driving without insurance in Spain is a serious offence for which you can be imprisoned. You must carry your insurance with you when driving or risk being fined. Drivers are legally required to have a minimum of third party insurance (*responsabilidad civil obligatoria*). Premiums tend to be reasonable, although the no claims bonus (*bonus malus*)

is usually not as good as in the UK.

If you have an accident, you must inform your insurance company quickly (usually within a couple of days). Fill in an accident report form (*declaración de siniestro de automóvil*) and return it as soon as possible.

Driving Tips
- The Spanish drive on the right.
- Give way to vehicles on the left.
- Seat-belts must be worn at all times in both front and back seats.
- Children under 12 must travel in the back if there is no suitable car seat or belt in the front.
- Road tax (*impuesto de circulación*) is payable annually on all vehicles with Spanish plates.
- Thanks to the siesta (3 to 5 p.m.) Spain has four rush hours (*horas puntas*): 8 to 9.30 a.m., 12.30 to 2.30 p.m., 3.30 to 4 p.m. and 6.30 to 8 p.m.
- On-the-spot fines can be imposed for offences such as speeding, although if you are a Spanish resident, you will probably be given time to pay. Non-residents, however, may be escorted to a bank. If you can't pay, your car may be impounded.

Public transport

On the whole, public transport in Spanish cities is cheap and efficient, with well-integrated bus and train services, and sometimes tram or underground lines, too. However, it's our experience that once you get outside the cities, the services are not as reliable, so leave plenty of time for your journey.

Useful information
- The same ticket can be used for all transport services.
- Commuter and visitor tickets are available.

- Students and pensioners are usually eligible for discounts.

Trains

Rail services are run by RENFE, and the jewel in their crown is the *tren de alta velocidad española* (AVE), a high-speed train that can take you from Madrid to Seville (a distance of 417 km) in two hours.

There are also many other types of train, with different fares, speeds and services. These include:

Cercanía: local commuter trains
Regionale: intercity trains
Largo recorrido: long-distance express trains, more expensive than the regionales (Advance booking is necessary for these.)

Note: RENFE's centralized booking service (see page 155) is staffed by English speakers.

Buses

Bus services run from around 6 a.m. until between 10 p.m. and midnight, when a night service normally comes into operation. At peak times buses on popular urban routes run every ten minutes.

Long-distance buses are clean, air-conditioned and a good way to see the country. You can buy tickets at machines or the ticket office at bus stations, or from the driver.

Internal flights

Iberia and Air Europa operate internal flights within Spain. Although quicker than express trains, they tend to be more expensive. Book early for cheap deals (see page 155).

Get a Life

Spaniards are sometimes disparaging about the Brits who arrive in vast numbers on their shores. They tend to see us as pasty-faced drunkards who are either face down on a beach or face down in a gutter. Perhaps it is because they are so proud of their country that they resent the fact that so many of us want to see no more of it than the beaches and the bars.

For our part, Brits can't reconcile the laid-back *mañana* and siesta side of Spain with all that macho bullfighting and frenzied flamenco dancing.

Making friends

Spaniards tend to be friendly and gregarious and will respond favourably to any efforts you make to integrate into their community – especially by speaking their language. Your local community will provide the richest source of potential friends – neighbours, shopkeepers, parents at the school gates… Sports clubs and social clubs are other obvious starting points.

Expats

At its best, the expat community can be a valuable source of information and support. At its worst … well, we all remember *El Dorado*. But at some time everyone craves a familiar language, a shared cultural reference and a warm beer with beans on toast and HP sauce.

Expat communities are particularly vibrant on the coasts and in the main cities. Contact the local British Consulate for a list of British clubs, societies and favourite meeting places. There may be a local English-language newspaper, school or 'Genuine British Pub' – all good starting points for meeting fellow Brits.

In remote regions, where there are few if any other expats, make use of the Internet for expat support. There are loads of chat rooms and websites offering a chance to swap experiences and get advice on every aspect of life in Spain.

Steps to Social Success

- When you're introduced to a Spaniard, shake hands and say good day (*buenos días*) or good evening (*buenas tardes*).
- It is considered rude to be any more than 15 minutes late for an appointment or invitation.
- Spaniards value neighbourliness and generosity as a national pastime; watch them fight over who is to pay a restaurant bill.
- Family and community are prized and fiercely guarded.
- Humour is different in Spain, and British sarcasm and irony can appear rude.
- Mañana is a way of life, so you'd better get used to it. Getting uptight won't make things happen any faster.

Shopping

With the exception of markets, where haggling is expected, retail prices are fixed in Spain and shown as PVP (*precio de venta al público*). Good buys include clothes and craft items (*artesanía*), and there is a thriving market in second-hand furniture.

Opening hours

Small shops are open Monday to Friday from 8.30 or 9.30 a.m. until 1 or 2 p.m. and from 5 p.m. to 7.30 or 9 p.m. On Saturday they open from 9.30 a.m. until 2 p.m.

Large shops and supermarkets are open all day until between 8 a.m. and 10 p.m.

Some big department stores and hypermarkets also open on Sundays.

Markets usually trade between 8.30 a.m. and 2 p.m., either a couple of days a week in small towns, or Monday to Saturday in larger towns and cities.

Food

Food is generally cheaper than in the UK.

Eating out

The Spanish love going out. It's part of their culture to get dressed up in the evening and wander through the streets, seeing and being seen. The main meal is usually lunch, and supper tends to be late – 9.30 onwards. Cheap, good food is plentiful in Spain, especially if you go where the locals go.

No matter where you end up eating, you won't be able to get away from tapas, and who would want to? These small but delicious snacks – olives, meatballs, ham, salad, cheese … the list is endless – are served with drinks. In most places off the beaten track you will pay for your drinks and tapas when you leave.

Below is a brief guide to the different types of 'eatery' you will be tempted by.

Asador: A sort of carvery.

Bar: Serves light meals, including tapas, with drinks.

Cafeteria: A type of snack bar.
Restaurante: There are many different types of restaurant in Spain, from cheap and cheerful *bodegas* to five-star eateries.
Marisqueia: A posh fish restaurant.

Tipping in restaurants is usually expected to be 10%.

Going out to bars and clubs happens after supper, and in most big cities people won't start serious partying until after midnight.

Jill and Barrie Burgess love the Spanish culture:
'The Spanish have got life sussed. They know what is important – spending time with family, eating out. We eat out two or three times a week here. In Britain we were lucky if we ate out twice a month.'

Cinema

In Spain cinema tickets are surprisingly cheap. Most US-made films are dubbed into Spanish, but in big cities you should be able to find cinemas screening English-language films without the voice-over.

Fiesta

You will not be able to miss your local fiesta. Often part of religious festivals, fiestas can last for days: everyone is out on the street eating, drinking, dancing and performing whatever ritual is native to the area, from tomato-throwing to bull-running. Many use fiestas as an excuse to dress up in regional costume, and they are a fantastic affirmation of community spirit and local cultural pride.

Staying in touch

The Spanish postal service (*Correo*) is slower than that of the UK, so anything destined for foreign parts should be sent via airmail. Addresses on internal mail should include the five-digit postcode to hurry things along a little, but in our experience it doesn't seem to make any difference whether you use it or not.

To telephone Spain from the UK dial 00 34 and omit the first zero of the Spanish number.
To telephone the UK from Spain dial 00 99 44 and omit the first zero of the UK number.

Emergencies

Spain has various free numbers that you can telephone in the event of emergency.

Dial 091 for *policía naciónal* or 092 for *policía local* (see below); dial 061 for an ambulance; 080 for the fire brigade.

There are four different police forces:

Guardia Civil: Officers wear green uniforms and cover roads, countryside, villages, prisons, borders and the environment.
Policía Naciónal: Officers wear blue uniforms or plain clothes, and deal with crime in cities and major towns. They also administrate passports, ID cards, residence permits, etc.
Policía Local: Officers wear blue and white uniforms and deal with parking, traffic and local by-laws.
Policía Regional: Officers working in the regions of Catalonia, the Basque Country, Valencia and Galicia.

Spain is generally a safe society. The well-documented terrorist threat from ETA (the Basque separatist movement) lurks under the surface, but apart from that, petty crime – often linked to drugs – is more of an irritant than a major problem. Car crime is the major concern, so never leave valuables in your vehicle.

6

Italy

For many Brits who want to relocate, the dream of a picturesque, ramshackle cottage tucked away among olive groves in the rolling hills of Tuscany still holds true. Well, whatever your Italian fantasy, it's time to stop dreaming. You can make it a reality.

Italy, officially called the Italian Republic, was unified as recently as 1861; before then it was a series of independent states. The country is still characterized by fierce regionalism, with marked differences in dialect, cuisine and way of life. There is also a noticeable north–south divide: the north (everywhere above Rome in some people's estimation) is wealthier, more industrialized and, some would say, more sophisticated than the south. Northerners have a reputation for looking down on the poorer southerners, many of whom still struggle with low wages and high unemployment.

In the early 1920s Benito Mussolini formed the *Partito Nazionale Fascista* – the national fascist party. Backed by liberals, he was elected prime minister in 1921, and, in 1925, having changed the legal structure of the country and taken control of the press, he announced that Italy was now under an anti-democratic dictatorship. Hand in hand with Nazi Germany, he dragged Italy into World War II, but when it became clear that the war was not going well, Mussolini was overthrown. Only after the war, when democracy was restored, did Italy start to recover.

Even though political corruption and organized crime are still rife today, Italians rise above problems in the system, to the point where the national motto could be 'Eat, drink and be merry'. Every day, it seems, there are festivals and fiestas. Given the chance, Italians will celebrate anything. And then there's the culture… With artefacts from the Roman Empire to the Renaissance filling galleries to the brim, and architectural masterpieces in every major city, Italians have a cultural history that's the envy of the world. And, of course, Italian cuisine is justifiably legendary.

Throw in the beautiful landscape – from glittering azure lakes to lush orange groves, from verdant mountainsides to rolling fields of corn – and Italy really is a country to fall in love with.

Politics

Italy is a republic made up of 20 administrative regions (*regioni*). It has a president and a prime minister. Parliament consists of the Senate and the Chamber of Deputies, both elected partly directly and partly by regional proportional representation.

Italian postwar politics was, until recently, dominated by two main parties, the Italian Communist Party (PCI) and the Christian Democratic Party (DC). Then, at the beginning of the 1990s, the PCI became the Democratic Party of the Left (PDS). The DC, plagued by controversy, was replaced by the Italian Popular Party (PPI), which has since fallen into virtual oblivion. As a result, party politics has polarized into left and right, with the centre practically disappearing.

Italy has a long and murky tradition of political corruption, which is, to many people, personified by Prime Minister Silvio Berlusconi, thought to be the richest man in Italy, with a business empire that includes newspapers, television, radio, football and advertising. But these business interests have led to scandals that have tarnished his image. Most recently, he was in court for allegedly bribing judges, but the trial was stopped when he rapidly instituted special immunity laws to prevent a prime minister being charged with corruption while still in office.

Economy

The economy divides the country into two parts: the industrialized and affluent north, and the poorer, still almost feudal south, which suffers with an employment rate of around 20%. Major industries are tourism, iron and steel, clothes, textiles and footwear, food, cars and ceramics. Agriculture is also crucial to the Italian economy.

In recent years, both interest and inflation rates have been lowered, and the economy is relatively healthy, thanks to strict economic policies imposed by the government in line with European Monetary Union requirements. However, the Italian constitution gives workers the right to unionize and to strike, so unions are still powerful in Italy and all-out strikes still occur.

Currency

Like the French, Italians have embraced the euro, and also complained that prices have risen as a result.

Religion

With Italy being the home of the Catholic Church and the Pope, it is hardly surprising that an estimated 98% of Italians are Catholic. While the older population, particularly in the south, is still deeply religious, church attendance is falling, not least among Italy's youth. There is also a growing Muslim community throughout Italy, most of it African in origin.

Time difference

Italy is on Central European Time, which is one hour ahead of GMT. Daylight Saving Time, from the last Sunday in March to the last Sunday in October, is two hours ahead of GMT (one hour ahead of British Summer Time).

Climate

From the alpine north to the dusty south, Italy's climate is generally kind, with hot summers and mild winters. In July the average temperature is around 30ºC (80ºF), dropping to an average 10ºC (50ºF) in January.

Brits in Italy

Brits tend to be well integrated into Italian society, making the most of what can be a more relaxed pace of life, with an emphasis on the family and quality of life. Although British expats can be found in all regions of Italy, the largest community of them is in Tuscany. It's not called Chiantishire for nothing.

Love/Hate

'You can eat like a king for next to nothing. A really good meal in a *trattoria* costs little more than a fiver.'

'There are a million reasons to move to Italy. The biggest one has to be the weather. It's gorgeous, gorgeous, gorgeous!'

'If you ask me, Italy has the most beautiful countryside in the whole of Europe. I was bitten by the "Italian bug" as soon as I got here.'

'There is so much bureaucracy. You need documents for everything. The red tape takes forever.'

'We live in a remote area of Tuscany, and although everyone is really friendly, no one speaks much English and we don't speak much Italian, so it's hard to make deep friendships. But I suppose that's better in the cities, where more people will speak English.'

'Buying a run-down property is relatively cheap in the area of Umbria in which we live, but we didn't realize how much it costs to do up a place. We ended up paying double the original building quotes. It made a real dent in our budget.'

'On a domestic level, you wouldn't believe the amount of limescale in the water. I've never seen anything like it. In the end we bought a water-softening machine. And there are a few things I can't get hold of here, including brown sugar and anti-perspirant. And marshmallows… I would kill for a bag of marshmallows.'

Get There

You don't need a visa to enter Italy, but within eight days of arrival, you'll need to apply for your *permesso di soggiorno* (residence permit). Get a form from the *questura* (administrative police headquarters) and be prepared to wait as the process is s-l-o-w. You need to be seriously determined because it's tempting to throw in the towel after many exasperating hours at the police station being passed from pillar to post. But don't give up – you will eventually get your hands on your prize. The good news is that your permit is valid for five years.

You will need…
- Passport
- Three black-and-white passport photos
- A completed application form, available from the *questura*
- Proof of financial means, such as bank statements
- Proof of intended status, such as a letter of employment or acceptance to a college course
- Birth certificates for children under 18

Citizenship

Any EU national can apply for Italian citizenship after four years of residence in Italy. If you're married to an Italian citizen and live in Italy, you can apply for citizenship six months after your wedding; if you live elsewhere, you can apply after three years.

Applications should be made to the Minister of the Interior through the *comune* (town hall). As with most Italian bureaucracy, the process is not for the faint-hearted. It can take an age and requires you to fill in reams of seemingly useless documents.

Eilidh Smith and Mike Austin-Eames, who relocated to Italy with their children Louis and Sam, have found that it's also important to research the procedure in the specific area you are moving to:

'When we first came here, we moved to Lucca. We went straight to the *questura* and were given a temporary *permesso di soggiorno* while our permanent one came through. We now live in Pescia and there isn't a *questura*. Apparently people have to send away for their *permesso*. I would strongly advise anyone thinking of doing what we have to try and get an idea of how the system works in the area of the country to which they are moving. It would make things much easier if people had an idea of the timescale for sorting out all the bureaucracy.'

Residency

If you are renting or have bought a house in Italy, you will be eligible for a *certificato di residenza* (certificate of residence). You can get one from the town hall.

Note: Before you sign a rental contract, it is a good idea to ensure that it doesn't state that you can't use your address to gain a certificate of residence. Some landlords include this clause as it makes eviction easier.

You will need…
- Passport
- *Permesso di soggiorno*
- Declaration from your country of origin's consulate in Italy confirming your details – name, parents' names, place and date of birth, civil status (married, divorced, or whatever) and nationality
- Completed *dichiarazione di residenza* (declaration of residence form), available from the town hall.

Guess what? Getting your *certificato di residenza* can takes ages. But residence status entitles you to most of the rights enjoyed by Italian nationals and is well worth having.

Pets

To take a cat or dog into Italy you need to get a Certificate of Health in English and Italian from a British vet registered with the Department of Food and Rural Affairs (DEFRA). The certificate is to show that Rover or Kitty is free from symptoms of disease. Dogs have to be immunized against rabies, hepatitis, kennel cough and distemper. Cats must be vaccinated against rabies, typhus and feline gastroenteritis. Certificates are valid for 30 days.

Puppies and kittens under 12 weeks are exempt from vaccinations, but you must obtain a health certificate (see above) and another certificate from a vet stating that the area from which the animal comes is rabies-free.

Your pets will not have to spend time in quarantine, but dogs are legally required to be tattooed as a means of registration, which must be done by a vet.

There are several animal diseases in Italy that are not found in other European countries. Ask your Italian vet for details and preventive measures. Vets' fees tend to be high, even for routine check-ups, so if you want to avoid hefty bills when things go wrong, we strongly recommend you take out some form of pet health insurance.

A scatological warning: although it is illegal to let your dog foul the street in most Italian towns and cities, many Italian pet owners tend to ignore the law. So watch where you tread, as it's all too easy to step in something unpleasant.

Your car

EU citizens can take their cars into Italy with no restrictions. You will be given a document called a *bolletta doganale* (customs pass) when your car clears customs, which allows you to drive legally.

Before you leave for Italy, make sure you have prepared your car as recommended in the EU section (see pages 36–7).

When you're there
If you're staying for six months or longer, you have to register your car with the *motorizzazione civile* (the equivalent of the DVLA), after which, you'll be given Italian plates. You can register your car in Italy if:

* You are an EU citizen
* You have a *residenza normale* in the country, i.e. if you live in Italy for at least 183 days of the year.
* You own a house or flat in Italy
* You have rented a house or flat in Italy for the last four years

Before being registered, your car will have to undergo a *collàudo* (official inspection). Take your car and your *bolletta doganale*, which you received at customs, to a *pratiche auto* (car documentation agency); you should be able to find at least one in every town. You can also register your car through the *Automobile Club d'Italia* (ACI) or the *Ufficio della Motorizzazione* (the official body dedicated to car registration). The number plates you are given remain valid as long as you have the car.

Remember, any driving licence issued within the EU is acceptable in Italy for as long as it is valid. However, 18 is the minimum driving age, so 17-year-olds with British licences will have to be patient.

Change of car ownership is called *passaggio di proprietà* and must be registered within ten days. The ACI and most car dealerships can handle this procedure for you for a small fee.

The Italian equivalent of the MOT does not kick in until a vehicle is ten years old. Thereafter, it must be inspected every two years.

Other belongings
EU nationals can take personal goods into Italy tax and duty free. However, you must make a detailed inventory of your belongings, with either a receipt or an approximate value in euros for each item.

To get household goods through Italian customs you will need a *codice fiscale* (fiscal code number), which is similar to a National Insurance number. For this, apply in writing to the Italian Consulate in London (see page 156). Include details of your name, place and date of birth, and your UK address, plus a copy of the relevant pages of your passport that show these details and your signature. Married women must also enclose certified copies of their birth and marriage certificates.

If you employ a removal company to take goods through customs in your absence, give them copies of your inventory, passport and *codice fiscale*. The firm will then be able get your goods through customs with no duty.

The electricity supply is 220 volts, which means things such as hairdryers work slightly slower. You'll just need new plugs and a screwdriver.

Get a Home

It's common knowledge that house prices in areas popular with Brits – especially Tuscany and Umbria – have rocketed in recent years. Prices are now bordering on the ridiculous, unless you have seriously deep pockets. Prospective buyers are now house-hunting in the less fashionable Marche and remote Puglia, but get in quickly, as there are fewer and fewer bargains to be had.

If moving to a city, you'll be gobsmacked by how small properties are. Most people live in two-bedroom apartments, and anything bigger is relatively rare because it costs so much. Of course, houses in cities are downright exorbitant.

Renting

Accommodation agencies and estate agents (*agenzia immobiliare*) advertise their services in local papers and the *Yellow Pages* (*Pagine Gialle*). Most newspapers have a section advertising accommodation to let (*appartamenti da affittare*). You can also spot property to rent when you are out and about by a 'to let' (*affittasi*) sign.

Many new arrivals stay in apartment hotels (*residenze ed appartamenti immobilati*), which are generally leased for a month at a time. These are listed in the Yellow Pages under '*Alberghi*'.

Generally speaking, you'll find that the further out of town you live, the cheaper the rent. However, one important thing to remember is that to rent accommodation in Italy you have to register your presence at the town hall.

Always remember to get an inventory of furnishings, itemizing everything in the property and its condition. Check it carefully before you sign the contract.

In Italy, most rental properties are let unfurnished (*non-ammobiliato*), which means you get the bare bones – walls, floors, wires, pipes and perhaps a bathroom. You will have to put in your own kitchen, carpets and everything else. Renter beware! Make sure you know exactly what you'll be provided with before you sign anything. You will save considerable disruption and expense if you can arrange to buy the outgoing tenant's cupboards, lights and kitchen fittings … unless they're horrible, of course. Then you'll have to make an emergency dash to Ikea.

Renting a room

If you're on your own and just want to rent a room, make sure you know the different terms for your own room (*càmera* or *stanza*) and a shared room (*posto letto*).

As in Britain, you'll probably have to come up with one month's rent in advance as a deposit (*cauzione*).

Repairs

The general rule in Italy is that tenants pay for minor repairs – a broken kitchen cupboard door, for example – and landlords meet the cost of major work (electrics, roofing, and so on). Difficulty can arise if there is a dispute about whether a problem with an appliance is caused by old age or previous maintenance (the landlord's responsibility), or wear and tear (the tenant's responsibility). We've found it best to insist on a clause being included in the contract, stipulating that in case of such disputes, a qualified repairman will be brought in to settle the issue. Don't sign a contract that doesn't have this provision – you'll regret it.

Payments

If you use an agency to find your accommodation, you will probably have to pay a fee of around a month's rent when you sign the contract. Rent is usually paid quarterly, and you'll be asked for 2–3 months' rent as a deposit. This means you'll have to part with up to four months' rent in advance, so make sure your budget can stand it.

Rental contracts

There are two kinds of contract:

Contratto di libero mercato (free-market contract) – this lasts four years and is renewable for another four years. The landlord and tenant agree terms between them.

Contratto convenzionale (standard contract) – this lasts three years and is renewable for two years.

You can give three or six months' non-renewal notice (*disdetta*). Note that if you fail to do so, your contract will be renewed as a matter or course. To make sure you aren't caught out, you must always send your *disdetta* by registered post and ask in the post office for a return receipt.

In our experience, it's best to get resident status in Italy because this, subject to conditions, protects you against eviction.

Property tax

You'll have to come up with half the local tax (*tassa di registro*), the equivalent of council tax. Your landlord pays the rest.

Buying

If you are thinking of buying in Italy, you can do a lot of research on the Internet (see page 156).

Italy has several real-estate publications, which specialize in certain types of property or parts of the country. These include *Casa e Casali* (farmhouses), *Porta Portese* and *Wanted in Rome* (Rome), *Secondamano* (Florence, Bologna and Milan) and *La Pulce* (Florence).

If you want to buy in Italy, you must always employ a lawyer, who should be registered with the official body, the *Ordine degli Avvocati*. For a list of English-speaking lawyers, contact your nearest British consulate in Italy.

Fees

Using professionals in Italy is expensive, and you can expect to pay a total fee of around 10% of the property's value for the services of an estate agent and lawyer. Good ones, however, are worth their weight in gold. Ask other expats for recommendations. You will also have to cough up 10% IVA (VAT) on a house.

The process

As with everything in Italy, buying a house means negotiating a bewildering labyrinth of bureaucracy, but fear not. Here is a simplified guide to the system.

If you are buying through an estate agent, you may be asked to make an official offer to purchase, which means you are bound to the offered amount for a particular period of time, usually either 14 or 30 days. If accepted, a deposit (usually 10%) is paid, followed by a further payment of 20–30% when the preliminary contract (*compromesso*) is signed. This means you lose your deposit if you back out.

Make sure the contract includes a clause stating that if the seller backs out, you will be entitled to a refund of double the deposit – standard practice in Italy. The transaction will then be handled by a public official called a *notaio*, who will execute the deed on behalf of both the seller and the buyer. A lawyer is essential to look after your interests while the transaction is going through.

The final transfer deed is called the *rògito*. The buyer must also pay a property registration fee and a land registry tax, plus the balance of the agreed price. Ask your lawyer for advice.

Before signing

Always hire an expert to research your chosen property. Unrenovated rural properties often lack water and power supplies, so get this checked out and remember that installing them can be a major expense. Also check out road access: you can't do up your dream home if materials can't be delivered.

You will need to get planning permission (apply at the town hall) for anything more than minor changes to a property and, of course, you'll be required to pay a fee.

To lessen the chances of costly disasters, we recommend that you use only licensed architects and tradesmen. Architects should be registered with the Ordine degli *Architetti*, and builders with the *Ordine degli Inegneri* (a register of civil engineers). They may be more expensive, but they'll save you money in the long run.

Mortgages

Estate agents can arrange your mortgage (*mutuo ipotecario*), but you could also approach one of the usual range of banks, high-street lenders and brokers. Inevitably, it takes ages to have a mortgage approved by an Italian bank, so be prepared for a long wait.

How large a mortgage can I get?

Mortgage repayments are usually limited to no more than 30% of your monthly income. Lenders will loan you up to 85% of the value of your first property (up to 95% if your home needs renovating) and up to 50% for your second home.

How is income calculated?

For mortgage purposes, your income can be calculated on single or joint earnings. Check with a mortgage adviser to find out which is best for you.

What if I'm not employed?

You might have trouble getting a mortgage if you don't have proof of a regular income. If you're self-employed, you will need to show your last tax return and your accounts for the last three years.

When do I arrange a mortgage?

Usually you get a mortgage when the first stage of the buying process is complete. The deposit required on signing the preliminary contract is protected by law if you don't then get a mortgage. It is possible to arrange a mortgage in advance, valid for up to four months, which will guarantee a mortgage up to an agreed sum, subject to a valuation of the property.

How long will it take?

Italian lenders are notoriously slow, so it might be quicker to arrange a mortgage through a foreign lender. Again, seek independent advice on which mortgage is best for you.

Are there any charges?

Lenders tend to charge an arrangement fee of around 1% of the loan. You will also have to budget for a registration tax of 2% and an administration fee of another 1%. Most lenders will also charge a fixed fee of around €100 for their services.

What types of mortgage are available?

You won't be able to get an endowment mortgage. Italians with a mortgage have to repay capital and interest.

Connecting utilities

To set up utility services, look in your local phone book under '*Numeri di Pubblica Utilità*' for the number of each service. Ask each utility company for the *servizio nuovo contratto* (new contract department).

Ente Nazionale per l'Energia Elettrica (ENEL) is the main electricity supplier in Italy, but other suppliers are available, depending on where you live. When you buy or rent a new property you have to sign a contract at an office of your chosen company. You'll receive an estimated bill every two months. Your meter will be read twice a year and your next bill altered accordingly. ENEL prefer their customers to pay by direct debit, but you can also pay at post offices, banks and company offices.

Societa Italiana per il Gas (ITALGAS) supplies mains gas. Contact your local office (see phone book) to have the meter read and your name put on to the account when you move into a property. You will receive a bill every two months, which can be paid by direct debit as well as at banks, post offices and ITALGAS offices.

Water is supplied by local companies (see phone book) and is usually metered. You'll generally be charged one rate for an annual limit, and another (higher) rate if you use more water than your limit. You will need a special contract to use water for your garden or swimming pool, which often costs an arm and a leg. Contact your local company when you move and they will read your meter and supply information about costs. You will get two bills a year. Payment can be arranged in the same way as other bills.

Telecom Italia organizes telephone installation. Go to the local office (see phone book) and fill in the relevant form. This will be in Italian, so if your grasp of the language is limited, take someone with you who can help. Also take your passport and a photocopy of it.

Peak times are Monday to Friday, 8 a.m. to 6.30 p.m. and Saturday, 8 a.m. to 1 p.m. Calls are cheaper on weekdays and Saturdays outside the peak period, and all day on Sunday and public holidays.

TV licence

You need a TV licence (*cànone televisivo*) in Italy, or you are liable to face prosecution. The annual licence currently costs €90.

Get a Job

Great news – if you're a national of any EU country, you can work wherever you want in Italy. But don't bank on it being easy to find a job. Unemployment is high, especially in the south.

Italy is the home of nepotism, and it still prevails in the job market today. Italians place a lot of importance on talking, and you'll be at a real disadvantage if you can't communicate at a reasonably sophisticated level. But don't be downhearted. If you have the necessary skills, lots of determination and fluent Italian, you will be able find that dream job.

Like everything in Italy, getting a job takes a long, long time – anything up to three months between applying and starting work.

Before you go

- Start looking for a job before you go. Your local Job Centre can give you advice about finding a job in Europe and whether you can continue to claim Job Seeker's Allowance for a time while you are there.
- Log on to the website of EURES, a Europe-wide job-listing service (see page 154).
- Don't forget to check whether your qualifications are recognized in Italy. For further information about this, see the EU section, page 37.
- Prepare a CV and keep it brief (two pages maximum).

Once you arrive

If you are hoping to work in Italy, you have to register at a government employment service office (*uffici di collocamento*). You'll need to take your residence permit with you.

A worker's registration card (*libretto di lavoro*) is required for most types of work. Apply to the *Inspettorato Provinciale del Lavoro*.

Jobs are advertised in the *lavoro* (work) section of regional and national newspapers. Vacancies are also held by job centres, called *Seziona Circoscrizionale per l'Impiego e il Collocamento in Agricoltura* (SCICA). These are run by government employment agencies (*Ufficio di Collocamento Mandopera*). There aren't many private employment agencies in Italy.

Interviews

Dress to impress at an interview – you can bet your bottom dollar everyone else will. Clothes and style are really important to Italians, and unless you are dressed to the nines, you may be overlooked.

Manners are also important. Don't sit down until you are asked to do so, don't criticize anyone, especially former employers, and for goodness' sake don't mention money until you feel you are close to being offered a job. Discussing salary at the first interview is an absolute no-no.

In general, there are more interviews during the selection process than in Britain – three or four interviews are far from unusual.

Accepting a job

Before accepting a job, you must have the agreement (*nulla osta*) of the public employment service. This applies even if you've found the job yourself through contacts or advertisements.

Although under EU law you shouldn't need a work permit, we've found that in Italy you probably will. When you've accepted a job, go to the *questura* and ask for a *permesso di soggiorno motivi di lavoro*.

You will need…

- Your passport
- A copy of your passport's data pages
- Two photos
- A letter from your future employers, stating that they intend to hire you and what your job will be.

Working conditions

Some companies, and many shops, break for a siesta. Most companies operate between 8.30 a.m. and 1 p.m. then 3 p.m. and 7 p.m. However, some, especially in the north, now work from 9 a.m. to 5 p.m.

Punctuality is less important in Italy than in some other countries. Chatting seems to be built into the working day, but you will be expected to make up any lost time.

Remember, don't pull out all the stops clothes-wise for your interview and then turn into a scarecrow when the job is yours. Unless you're doing manual labour, you'll be expected to be neat and well dressed at all times. Of course, this being Italy, and style being a part of the national psyche, the definition of 'well dressed' changes constantly.

Italy has no national minimum wage, though some professional bodies set their own minimum wage every three years.

There is a maximum 48-hour week. Overtime, which is not compulsory, is usually paid at up to one-and-a-half times the normal hourly rate.

Annual holidays, excluding the ten public holidays, are usually around 25–30 days per year.

At Christmas, most employees receive extra money called the *tredicesima mesilità* (13th-month salary) or the *gratifica natalizia* (Christmas bonus).

Hardly anyone works weekends, apart from where it can't be avoided, such as in shops and restaurants.

Employment contracts

Italian law states that every employee must have a contract. Always insist that your employer gives you a written contract, with an English translation if your Italian isn't up to scratch so that you can ensure you understand every word before you sign. The principal types of contract are as follows:

Dipendente – for employees
Contratto di appredistato – for apprentices
Lavoro stagionale – for seasonal workers
Lavoro interinale – to cover absences, such as maternity leave.

Contracts are either permanent (*contratto a tempo indeterminato*) or temporary and for a fixed term (*contratto a tempo determinato*).

Self-employment

Setting up in business is always complicated, and in Italy the bureaucracy is a nightmare. We recommend that you hire the services of a lawyer to make sure you don't fall at the first hurdle, and to choose one used to dealing with expats so that they are aware of issues that might affect you.

If you want to set up your own company, you have to register with the local Chamber of Commerce (*Camera di Commercio*). You must also have your *permesso di soggiorno* changed to a *permesso di soggiorno per lavoro autonomo/indipendente*. You are also obliged to register with the local tax office (*intendenza di finanza*).

You will have to get a codice fiscale, which is issued by the *Agenzia delle Entrate* (the local inland revenue office, see page 156) and requires some form of ID.

You can also ask the British Embassy in Rome (see page 156) or a British consulate to submit your request to the *Agenzia delle Entrate*. Alternatively, the Italian Consulate in London can grant power of attorney to someone living in Italy so that they can request a *codice fiscale* on your behalf.

Get Healthy

The national health service situation in Italy is like that in many European countries – the system is sophisticated but overstretched. However, waiting lists do tend to be shorter than in Britain. Care tends to be patchy and facilities are generally better in the more affluent north.

Italy's version of the NHS is the *Servizio Sanitario Nazionale* (SSN). This covers:

- Hospitalization
- GP and specialist treatment
- Prescription medicines
- Tests
- Maternity services
- Ambulances for emergencies and transfers between SSN hospitals.

National health insurance

If you are resident in Italy, you are eligible for national health insurance (*mutua*). (If you are working, your employer will pay a proportion of the fees for you.) To register, go to your nearest local health authority office, *Azienda Sanitaria Locale* (ASL).

You will need...
- Passport
- *Permesso di soggiorno* and residence certificate
- Family status certificate (*certificato di stato di famiglia*), available from the town hall,

if you want to register your children or spouse
- *Codice fiscale*

You will be given a booklet (*libretto sanitario*) to prove you are registered. Like your residence permit, this registration document will last for five years.

Private health care

There are various private health insurance companies in Italy. The biggest is Istituto Nazionale delle Assicurazioni. For your local branch, look under '*Assicurazioni*' in the *Yellow Pages*.

Alhough it goes without saying that private hospitals tend to be more luxurious than state ones, there tends to be little difference in standards of medical treatment. Private hospitals are listed in the *Yellow Pages* under '*Case di cura private*'.

Getting a GP

When you apply for health insurance (national *and* private), you will have to choose a doctor from an official list. Once you are registered and have started your payments, visits to your chosen doctor should be free.

Hospitals

In an emergency, go to the A&E department (*pronto soccorso*) of the nearest hospital. Otherwise, you will be treated by a hospital only if referred by a doctor.

Pharmacies

Pharmacies, indicated by a green or red cross, tend to be family-run businesses. They are usually open Monday to Friday, 8.30 a.m. to 12.30 p.m. and 4 p.m. to 8 p.m., and Saturdays, 9 a.m. to 12 p.m. Details of the nearest 24-hour pharmacy will be displayed on the door, or advertised in local newspapers.

If you are registered with social security, you will have to pay a percentage towards the cost of prescription medicines. The percentage is determined according to the type of drug prescribed.

Dentists

Dentists aren't covered by health insurance, and fees can be seriously hefty, so remember to ask for a receipt as some dental expenses are tax-deductible.

Get Wealthy

This section fills you in on handling your finances in Italy, covering everything from banks and bills to taxes and wills.

Banks

There are three kinds of banks in Italy – commercial banks, co-ops and co-op credit banks, which are small independent banks owned and run locally. Major banks include

Banca di Roma, Banca Commerciale Italiana and Banca Nazionale del Lavoro.

Many Italian banks still have relatively high rates of interest, so make sure you really shop around before deciding where to borrow.

Opening a bank account

It is not essential to be a resident in order to open a bank account, but the rules vary, so check out your options in advance.

You will need…

- Proof of identity, such as a passport or driving licence
- Proof of your address, such as a utility bill
- *Codice fiscale*
- Some banks may ask for a residence permit – check before you go.

Cheques

When filling in cheques use only blue or black ink. Write *non trasferibile* (not transferable) on the cheque. This is the equivalent of crossing it.

When you are writing numbers on cheques, make sure you use the correct punctuation: Italians use a full stop where we might put a comma, and a comma where we would put a full stop. For example, where we'd write 3,400.20, an Italian would write 3.400,20. When writing the amount, the words should all be connected and contain no capital letters.

Interest is withheld on cheques starting from the date on the cheque, not from the date of the transaction, so you may be given cheques with the date space blank and be trusted to fill it in on the day you cash it.

It is a criminal offence to write a cheque if you don't have the funds to cover it.

Withdrawing cash

Withdrawal slips aren't used in Italy. You have to write a cheque made out to yourself – *me stesso* for men, *me stessa* for women. You

can usually withdraw cash by cheque only in your own branch. You will be charged for cheque books and for each cheque written.

You can also withdraw cash from machines using your Bancomat card (like Switch). You will be charged (usually €1) when you withdraw cash from another bank's machine. You can also use your card to pay for goods at many shops and supermarkets. Credit cards are widely used.

Bank charges

Expect bank charges to be pretty steep. With most banks in Italy you have to pay for cheque books, each cheque you write and every transaction over a certain limit (usually 100 transactions per year).

Bank statements

Bank statements are issued monthly or every four months – you should be able to choose which.

Banking hours

Although hours vary, banks generally tend to open Monday to Friday, 8.30 a.m. to 1.30 p.m. and 2.30 to 4.30 p.m.

Taxes

Tax is a specialist area, so always take advice from an expert. You really don't want to be landed with a massive bill by suddenly discovering you've not paid all the tax you should.

Income tax (*Imposta sul reddito delle persone fisiche*)

Italy has a pay-as-you-earn system, known as '730', after the relevant form. In most cases, this form covers all personal deductions applicable to individuals. Your employer will ask you for the relevant information to sort this out and deduct a monthly amount for tax.

If your tax situation is more complicated, you'll have to file an additional tax return (*modello unico*). You will have to pay income tax in Italy if:

- You spend 183 days or more in Italy in one year
- Your permanent or principal residence is in Italy
- Your main source of income, investment or business is in Italy

Property tax (*Imposta comunale sugli immobili*)

Known for short as ICI, this tax must be paid to the local council and is levied on any land or property you own in Italy, whether or not you are resident there. It is charged at anything between 0.4 and 0.7% of the value of your property or land. If your property is unfit for habitation, the amount you pay is halved.

Value added tax (*Imposta sul valore aggiunto*)

IVA is around 20% and is included in the price of goods in shops. You will have to register for VAT only if you are self-employed or own a business.

Capital gains tax (*Imposta comunale sull'incremento di valore degli immobili*)

The capital gain on the sale of a property is taxed at 3–30%. This is reduced by half if the property is your principal residence. Capital gains tax is also levied on stocks and shares.

Social security

Refer to the EU section (page 38) for details.

Pensions

If you are working, state pension contributions should be automatically paid on your behalf. Make sure your employer gives you an annual certificate showing what has been paid.

As in the UK, the state pension may not be worth much by the time you retire, so you need to give serious consideration to taking out a private pension.

The self-employed must join a state pension scheme, and have to pay their own contributions, roughly 16% of the previous year's declared income. Contributions are tax-deductible.

Wills

The nub of wills in Italy is the question of where you were resident at the time of death. If you weren't an Italian resident, your estate can be disposed of according to a will made under the law of the country in which you were resident. There are three types of will in Italy:

Holographic will – no witnesses are needed and it costs nothing to draw up, so this is the most widely used type of will. It must be done in your own handwriting, including the date and your signature.

Public will – prepared by a notary and witnessed by two people.

Secret will – rarely used, this is written by a testator or third party and given to the notary already sealed.

Get Wise

State education from nursery to university is more or less free for everyone in Italy. Education is compulsory for children aged six to fifteen.

There are several international schools in Italy, mainly in the big cities. Most international schools teach in English. For information contact the British Embassy (see page 156).

You can get information about schools in your area from the town hall or *provveditorato* (local education office). Italian schools don't operate catchment areas. To enrol your child at an Italian school contact your local town hall.

You will need…
- A translation of qualifications (exam certificates), if applicable
- A letter from your child's previous head teacher translated into Italian
- Child's birth certificate
- Proof of immunizations
- Photo of child
- Your residence permit
- Family status certificate (*certificato di stato di famiglia*) available from the town hall.

Italy's education system
Here's a quick rundown of what you can expect to encounter when you dip a toe into Italy's education system.

Pre-school, ages 3–6 (*Materna*)
Nearly all Italian children attend some sort of pre-school institution, as Italy's pre-schooling is excellent. Children learn through play, and there is no formal reading or writing until children start primary school. State-run and private facilities are available.

Primary school, ages 6–11 (*Scuola elementare*)
Most primary-aged school children attend class in the mornings for five days a week, with just a couple of afternoon classes. Primary teaching is divided into two distinct stages. The basics of reading and writing are prioritized in the first two years, with science, history and other disciplines being introduced in the final three years.

Middle school, ages 11–15 (*Scuola media*)
At the end of middle school, pupils sit a state exam that includes written and oral sections. Those who pass can go on to secondary school.

Secondary school, ages 15–19 (*Scuola superiore*)
Pupils attend *liceo* (grammar school) or *instituto tecnico* (technical college), depending on their particular aptitudes. While tuition is still free for children aged 15 and upwards, parents have to pay enrolment taxes – not a steep outlay. They must also buy school books and stationery. At the end of secondary school, pupils sit the *diploma di maturita* (upper secondary school diploma).

Private education
While private schools do exist in Italy, the education pupils receive isn't regarded as any better than state education.

School year
The school year consists of three *trimestri* (terms), the dates of which vary between regions. The first term runs from mid-September to mid-December, the second from early January to mid-March, and the third from early April to early June.

The school week is Monday to Saturday. Lessons in most primary schools run from 8 a.m. to 1 p.m., with afternoon classes until 4 p.m. about twice a week. Lessons at middle and secondary schools last from 8.15 a.m. to around 1.30 p.m.

Learning the language
It can't be stressed enough – you *must* learn Italian before you go. Enrol at evening classes, have private lessons, buy a course of tapes – anything that will give you a working knowledge of the language.

Once in Italy, you can also attend one of the language schools that are dotted all over the place.

Get Around

Travelling in Italy is unpredictable to say the least. In the cities, particularly in the north, roads and public transport, especially trains, are slick, well maintained and efficient. In rural areas and large parts of the south, however, bus and train services are patchier, and some roads are barely worthy of the name.

Driving Tips
- Italians drive on the right.
- Give way to vehicles coming from the right at junctions.
- Seatbelts and child car seats are compulsory.
- The middle lane of a three-lane road is for overtaking.
- Using a mobile phone while driving is illegal unless you have hands-free speakers.
- Don't park in *zona di rimozione* (tow-away zones) in cities. Enforcement is fierce.
- Police can demand on-the-spot fines for violations. If you cannot pay, your car may be impounded.
- Look out for scooters and mopeds, which whizz around with apparently little regard for the rules of the road.
- The ACI (the Italian equivalent of the AA) runs breakdown services. Call 116 for assistance 24 hours a day.

On the road
The driving's fast and tempers do flare easily, but, contrary to popular belief, anarchy does not rule the roads in Italy.

Italian roads are generally well maintained, and there is an excellent network of *autostrada* (motorways). The latter operate tolls (*il pedaggio*) generally issuing a ticket as you enter and taking payment when you leave.

However, some motorways instead have fixed-price tolls at regular intervals. You can pay in cash or by credit card, or get toll cards from offices of the ACI, some bars and restaurants on the motorway and certain banks. There is also a system called Telepass, which involves an authorized technician installing a mechanism in your car to let you drive through specified Telepass gates and charges the tolls to your bank account. Ask about it at the ACI or your bank.

Take care not to lose your ticket or enter an *autostrada* without one. If you do, you will be charged for the longest possible distance on that particular motorway.

Insurance
Third-party insurance (*responsabilità civile*) is compulsory, and you should have this at the very least. Proof of up-to-date insurance cover must be shown on your windscreen. If you drive over Italy's borders, you must carry a green card that proves you have European insurance cover. Your insurer in the UK or Italy will be able to provide you with this.

Italian insurance companies operate a no-claims (*bonus-malus*) index, which operates in the same way as that in the UK.

Relatively few people have fully comprehensive insurance (*casco*) as it is so expensive. It's worth shopping around for your insurance policy because fees can vary wildly.

Carry the *constatazione amichevole* (friendly claim) form provided by your insurance company in your car at all times. If you have a minor accident with little damage and no injuries, you should use your form to record all the relevant details. It is also a good idea to carry a disposable camera to take photos of any damage caused to your car.

In the event of a more serious accident, call the police and don't forget to set up your emergency triangle markers.

Trains

Cheap, fast and efficient, trains are probably the best way to travel in Italy. Ferrovie dello Stato (FS – Italian State Railways) oversees around 3,500 stations, covering the greater part of the country. To ensure getting a seat, especially on Fridays and at weekends, a reservation can be made for a small fee.

Always stamp your train ticket before your journey at the yellow machine on the platform. If you forget, you risk being fined.

Twice yearly FS issues a timetable, '*In Treno in Tutt' Italia*', which gives details of major routes and can be obtained from railway station kiosks.

FS has a range of cut-price tickets, rail cards and special offers, so always explore the options before you buy, especially for long journeys.

Buses

In cities, buses are cheap and well run. You can buy tickets from tobacconists, newsagents and any shop with a sign saying *biglietti*. In rural areas, buses can be slow and erratic, to say the least. On Sundays, especially in the south, services are practically non-existent.

Bus terminals are called *autostazione*. You can buy tickets from the station or on the bus. Once on board, you must validate your ticket in the machine on the bus, or you may be fined.

Internal flights

Internal flights are expensive, although generally very quick. Airlines offering domestic flights include Aero Transporti Italiani, Alitalia and Aermediterranea.

Ferries

Italy's islands are all served by ferry or hydrofoil links to the mainland, and timetables change according to season. There are also ferry links between some towns on Italy's northern lakes.

Get a Life

The Italians really have got life sussed. Many begin their day with a visit to a bar for a pre-work breakfast of coffee and a pastry. Family life being all important means that everyone goes home for lunch, the main meal of the day, which is generally accompanied by a bottle or two of wine, followed by a civilized siesta. Work recommences for a few hours, then it's time for the evening meal, invariably with beer or more wine. Between lunch and dinner on Sundays Italians take to the streets for the *passeggiata*, the walk when they gossip and watch each other pass by.

The Italian lifestyle of eating, drinking and generally enjoying yourself is a great one, so when in Rome, do as the Romans do – it would be rude not to.

Making friends

Italians are generally friendly and hospitable. The best way to meet them is in bars and cafés, where drinks and meals are long and leisurely. Alternatively, just hang out in the town square and you are sure to meet someone only too willing to chat.

Eilidh and Mike have certainly found Italy a welcoming place to be:

'Even when you move house in the same area it takes a while for it to feel like home, so you have to expect mixed emotions when you've moved to a whole new country. You can't expect to feel settled and happy all at once. But Italy is great because the people here are so lovely. If you feel a bit low or homesick you can go into a shop or sit down for a coffee, and the people will be so kind to you that you instantly feel lifted.'

Steps to Social Success

- Italians place a lot of emphasis on family. Wherever you go you'll see huge extended families, from tiny babies to great-granny, enjoying each other's company.
- Older people are treated very respectfully in Italy, with elderly relatives being the centre of the family. Always be polite to older people, or risk being on the receiving end of the famous Italian fiery temper.
- When you are first introduced to someone you have never met before, it is usual to shake hands and say hello (*buon giorno* or *buona sera*). The more informal greeting *ciao* tends to be used only among close friends and youngsters.
- Most Italians kiss when they meet – once on the right cheek, once on the left. If you're not sure you know someone well enough to kiss, wait for them to make the first move.
- If you're offered a glass of wine with a meal, wait until your host has made a toast before getting stuck in.
- The Italians *adore* children. Your little darlings will be welcomed everywhere and treated like royalty.

Expats

If you want to meet fellow Brits, joining an expat club is probably the best bet. These social clubs can be found in most big towns and cities, and are advertised in English-language publications, such as *Grapevine*, *Informer*, *Hello Milano* and *Wanted in Rome*. You can also ask for details at the British Embassy or your local town hall.

Shopping

Italians are famed for their style. Anywhere more built up than two houses and a pigsty will have a spectacularly trendy clothes shop. You can worship at many fashion shrines – Gucci, Versace, Armani, Valentino – the list is endless. Italian interior design shops are rather tasty, too. However, prices are often ridiculous, so unless you have a huge budget, you might want to browse more often than buy.

Opening hours

As a general rule most shops are open Monday to Saturday, 9 a.m. to 1 p.m. and 3 to 7 p.m. for most of the year, but change during the summer, often at the whim of the owner, who might want to make the most of the fantastic weather. However, things are changing, and opening hours are generally quite regular.

Supermarkets outside major cities sometimes close on Monday mornings.

In large towns and cities, markets usually open Monday to Friday from early in the morning until around 1 p.m., and all day on Saturday. In smaller places markets tend to open a couple of mornings a week.

Food

Most Italians shop for food every day to make sure it is as fresh as possible. They also tend to prefer small shops to big supermarkets, believing that the produce is infinitely better than the vacuum-packed and shrink-wrapped stuff offered elsewhere.

So various are Italy's culinary delights that it's impossible to list them all. Look out for Parma ham, regional salamis, buffalo mozzarella and tomatoes that taste full of sun.

Eating out

Italy is a foodie's fantasy, with some of the tastiest grub in the world. Each region has its own culinary specialities, from wild boar in Piedmont to chillied squid in Sicily. For a really good meal, avoid the tourist spots and watch where the locals eat. Below is a brief guide to the different types of 'eatery' you will find:

Pizzeria: selling (what else?) pizza, you will find most pizzerias so cheap that you have to eat standing up, while others are expensive tourist hot-spots.

Ristorante: a more up-market version of a trattoria (see below).

Tavola calda: literally a 'hot table', this is a self-service cafeteria, ideal for cheap and cheerful lunches.

Trattoria: usually a family business, selling a variety of meals.

Smoking

Smoking is banned in public places, but the rules are often flouted.

Football

It's impossible to write about Italian life without mentioning *calcio* (football). It's a national passion: huge crowds gather at every match of the top clubs, and stadiums can be sold out for a season at a time. An Italian football match will be among the most exciting and noisiest experiences of your life. Be sure to go at least once.

Cinema

In Italy it is hard to find showings of foreign films in their original language; most are dubbed into Italian. Your best bet of seeing an English film in its original form is in a city, where there may be an English cinema or a cinema that shows films in English on certain days of the week.

Staying in touch

The Italian postal service (*La Posta Italiana*) is slow, slow, slow. Every property in Italy has a five-digit postcode and it's essential to use it if you want mail to arrive during your lifetime. If you want to receive mail before you have an address, it can be sent to your town's central post office (for a small fee). To pick it up you will probably need your passport.

The state telephone company, SIP, is responsible for public telephones. Some call boxes still take coins, but most use phone cards, available from bars and newsagents. (You have to tear off the perforated corner of the card before use.) Bars often have public phones. To ring home you can buy an international phone card, available from main post offices.

For information in English about telephone services call 800 020020 Monday to Friday, 8.30 a.m. to 4.30 p.m.

To telephone Italy from the UK dial 00 39 and omit the first zero of the Italian number.
To telephone the UK from Italy dial 00 44 and omit the first zero of the UK number.

Emergencies

Italy has various free numbers that you can telephone in the event of emergency.

Dial 112 for the *polizia di stato*; 113 for any general serious emergency; 118 for an ambulance; 115 for the fire brigade. There are several police forces in Italy:

Carabinieri are a branch of the army and deal with serious crime, including the mafia. They wear dark blue uniforms.

Guardia Finanza, the financial police, deal with fraud. They wear grey uniforms with yellow epaulettes.

Polizia di Stato are the national police force, responsible for dealing with traffic, thefts and other everyday criminal matters. They wear dark blue jackets and light blue trousers.

Vigili Urbani deal with traffic and local affairs. They wear a dark uniform with a white helmet.

7

Australia

Think of all the reasons you want to start a new life abroad. Endless sandy beaches? A more laid-back lifestyle? Year-round sunshine? Well, you can find all of these in Australia, often called the 'lucky country'. For stressed-out, sun-starved Brits, Australia really can be a little bit of heaven on Earth.

Anthropologists believe that Australia's first human inhabitants, the Aborigines, travelled to the continent from Asia around 50,000 years ago. The first European settlers arrived in 1778, initially to establish a British penal colony, but later to exploit the country's natural resources. During the 1850s Aboriginal people were driven from much of their land after the discovery of gold, and for many years afterwards suffered badly at the hands of the incomers. Modern Australia is struggling to come to terms with this part of its history, from which many Aborigines have still not recovered. Poverty and alcoholism among Aboriginal communities is higher than in any other section of society.

Australia became part of the Commonwealth in 1901, and continues to regard the British monarch as its head. In 1999 a referendum to decide whether the country should become a republic was defeated by 55% of the vote.

Australia is huge – 50% bigger than Europe – but has the lowest population density on the planet: only two people per square kilometre.

However, most people live in the conurbations of Sydney, Brisbane, Adelaide, Melbourne and Perth – some of the most vibrant and cosmopolitan cities in the world. Australians pride themselves on being a truly multicultural nation, with food and the arts displaying many influences. We're all familiar with Aussie slang, such as 'grog' (alcohol) and 'chook' (chicken), courtesy of television programmes such as *Neighbours*. But did you know that 'thongs' are flip-flops and 'bludger' means lazy? Alongside the Australian dialect, known as Strine, many Aboriginal dialects are also in regular use and gaining new respect.

The vast Australian terrain includes a bit of everything. Being the flattest country in the world, it has mile upon mile upon mile of open plain, but it also boasts spectacular mountain ranges, parched deserts and lush rainforests.

Politics

Australia is a federal democratic state, recognizing Queen Elizabeth II as sovereign, although she is a figurehead with no real constitutional powers. She is represented by the governor general. Australia has a two-tier government consisting of the Senate and the House of Representatives, both of which are elected by popular vote. There is currently a ruling Liberal Party/National Party coalition.

Australia is composed of six states – New South Wales (capital Sydney), Queensland (Brisbane), South Australia (Adelaide), Tasmania (Hobart), Victoria (Melbourne) and Western Australia (Perth) – and two territories: Australian Capital Territory (Canberra) and Northern Territory (Darwin). States and territories enjoy a large degree of autonomy.

Australia's prime minister is currently John Howard, the leader of the Liberal Party. He is in his third term, having been elected in 1996, 1998 and 2001. His party is currently in coalition with the conservative National Party, an alliance that won 43% of the vote at the last election.

Economy

Australia is one of the world's richest countries, its major industries being mining, food production, steel and chemicals. With a prosperous economy and low unemployment, Australia has so far escaped the worst effects of the worldwide economic slowdown. Unfortunately, its agriculture has been badly hit recently by the worst droughts in a century.

Currency

Australians use the Australian dollar ($A), nicknamed the 'buck'.

Religion

Seventy-five per cent of Australians consider themselves Christian, although nowhere near that amount are regular churchgoers. Australia's immigrant communities from South-east Asia mean that Buddhism and Islam are also widely practised.

Time difference

With Australia being so large, it has three time zones. For Western Australia add nine hours to GMT. For South Australia and the Northern Territory add nine-and-a-half hours. For Queensland, the Australian Capital Territory, Victoria and New South Wales add ten hours.

Between October and March, Daylight Saving Time is used in New South Wales, the Australian Capital Territory, Victoria and South Australia. This adds one hour to the time difference.

Climate

Australia is synonymous with beautiful sunny weather, the north being tropical, and the south temperate. Australian seasons occur at opposite ends of the year to those in the UK, with winter officially starting in June, and summer beginning in December. Most Aussies spend Christmas on the beach. But even in winter the Australian climate is kind, being generally warm, dry and sunny.

Over the last few years, Australia has suffered from extremely dry summers, which have dried out the bush, making it easier for fires to start – either naturally or by human hand. As a result, families who live on the edge of the bush are forced to take precautions, such as making sure trees are a specified distance from the house and that they have a pumping system in full working order so that they can use water from the swimming pool if the worst should happen.

Brits in Australia

Australia is one of the most popular destinations for migrating Brits, so there are thriving expat communities in most parts of the country. But many Australians (like many Brits) are firmly against immigrants, particularly those from 'poorer' countries, convinced that they merely want to scrounge off the state.

National stereotypes, not least 'whinging Poms', are a source of many barbed jokes. In fact, Brit-baiting is a national pastime. Brits, for their part, cannot resist reminding Australians of their convict past.

On the whole, however, Brits and Aussies get along quite well, united by their shared love of cricket and rugby and their common heritage.

Love/Hate

'Life isn't such a constant fight here as it is in Britain. People are polite and friendly and help each other out. There is no road rage and little crime.'

'Property is relatively cheap here. And you get so much more space for your money. Our house here is huge compared to our cramped three-bedroom semi back in the UK. The kids can even ride their bikes in the house. They can't believe their luck.'

'The national health system is second to none. Everything is clean, quick and efficient. Australia is the place to be ill!'

'Waiting to hear if your application for a visa has been passed is one of the most stressful experiences I've ever been through. We finally found out we'd been accepted 18 months after applying. Eighteen months in limbo – torture!'

'Vegemite – yuk! Whenever anyone from the UK comes to stay I tell them to load up with Marmite.'

'I miss my family terribly, and because it's so expensive for them to fly here and for me to fly to the UK, I don't get to see them half as much as I'd hoped I would.'

Get There

Want to live in Australia? Of course you do. But be prepared to negotiate a bureaucratic maze. The process is incredibly confusing, time-consuming and frustrating. Just be careful it doesn't make you crook (ill). To avoid this, we would strongly recommend that you spend the £600–£900 it takes to secure the skills of a professional migration agency to help you through the process. Under Australian law, anyone who provides immigration assistance must be registered with the Migration Agents' Registration Authority (MARA) (see page 156).

Getting your visa

All foreign nationals entering Australia need a visa, so make yourself a strong cuppa – you're going to need it.

Your first port of call should be the Australian government's Department of Immigration and Multicultural and Indigenous Affairs (DIMIA) (see page 156). Its easy-to-use websites give detailed information about visas, and more general hints about migrating to Australia. You can also download application forms and send off for essential booklets. Note that visa requirements change constantly, so we cannot over-emphasize the need to check with DIMIA before you start.

For the best chance of success, you must do in-depth research into the most appropriate visa for you, then think very carefully. Fees are hefty, and if your application fails or you change your mind and withdraw, you won't get your cash back.

There are two ways in for Brits looking to make a new life in Oz: the Skilled Migration Stream, for people who are highly talented, or with special work or business skills; and the Family Migration Stream, which allows people to be sponsored by a relative who already lives in Australia. However, within each of these two migration streams, there are several types of visa available. While it's not always immediately obvious which path will offer you the best opportunity, stick with the research. It will be worth it.

Skilled Migration Stream

The visas that fall within this category target anyone under 45 who has special talents or skills and will rapidly contribute to Australia's economy. Around 70% of Brits migrate under this scheme, and obtain an Offshore General Skilled Visa, available in the following types:

Skilled Independent Visa

Consider this option if you meet the following basic requirements:

- You must be under 45 years old.
- You must be able to show you have English language skills. An English language O-Level or GCSE is great, but if you don't have an English qualification – even if you're a native English speaker – you must sit a DIMIA English test.
- You must have university or trade qualifications. For a few jobs, a long period of work experience is enough. Check on the DIMIA website (see page 156) for more information.
- You must have your skills assessed by an appropriate Australian authority. Form 1121i gives details, including addresses, of whom you should approach. You'll need to send them your work documents, such as trade qualification certificates and references. The authority will decide whether your skills match their criteria. Be warned – this process can take several months, so it is wise to make this the first thing

you do in the application process.
- You must nominate an occupation from the Skilled Occupation List (SOL), form 1121i, available from the DIMIA websites. This is a list of jobs in demand in Australia. While it is always changing, there is a permanent need for hairdressers, air-conditioning and refrigeration technicians, some IT professionals and chefs.
- You must have relevant work experience.
- You must pass a points test to establish your desirability as an immigrant. The pass mark is currently 115 points, and these are awarded for:
  - Skill: the job you nominate on the SOL will be worth between 40 and 60 points.
  - Your age when you apply: those aged 18–29 get 30 points; 30–34 get 25 points; 35–39 get 20 points; 40–44 get 15 points.
  - English language ability is worth 15–20 points.
  - Work experience is worth 5–10 points.
  - If your occupation is currently classed as in demand, you'll gain points for this, and for any job offer in this class (10–15 points).
  - Having Australian qualifications confers 5–15 points. If you have lived and studied in a rural area of Australia or part of a city classed as having low population growth, you can gain an extra 5 points.
  - Spouse skills: if your spouse can satisfy all the basic requirements, you'll gain 5 points.

  Bonus points may be awarded for one of the following:
  - Investing at least A$100,000 in Australia.
  - Work experience in Australia in any occupation on the SOL for at least six months in the last four years.
  - Being fluent in an Australian community language apart from English. You have to

hold a post-secondary qualification in the language and be able to prove your course was taught in that language.

For more information about how you might score, read booklet six, 'General Skilled Migration', available from DIMIA and other migration websites (see page 156).

Skilled State Territory Nominated Independent Visa

The conditions for this type of visa are as follows:

- You must meet the basic requirements listed above for the Skilled Independent Visa.
- You must reach at least the 'pool' mark in the Skilled Independent Visa points test (the current 'pool' mark is 70).
- You must be nominated by a participating state or territory that can select people to fill job vacancies. For more information, go to the official website of the state that interests you.

Skill Matching Visa

While there is no charge for this type of visa – you pay a fee only if nominated for a job – most experts agree that skill matching is the last chance saloon in visa land. To qualify, you must meet the basic requirements listed above for the Skilled Independent Visa, then your name can be placed on an official skill-matching database for up to two years. This database is sent to state and territory governments to allow employers to fill vacant posts. If you haven't been chosen after two years, your application will be refused.

Family Sponsored Visa

This is *not* the Family Migration Stream. There are two categories of Family Sponsored Visa, as follows:

1. Skilled Designated Area Sponsored Visa

- You must satisfy the basic requirements listed above for the Skilled Independent Visa.
- You must have an assurer (an Australian citizen or permanent resident) who will agree to give you financial support.
- You or your spouse must be related to a sponsor who lives in one of the designated areas. The Australian High Commission will give you details about which areas are included. You or your spouse must be your sponsor's non-dependent child, parent, sibling, niece or nephew. Your assurer and sponsor can be the same person or different people.

2. Skilled Australian Sponsored Visa

- You must meet the basic requirements listed above for the Skilled Independent Visa.
- You must have an assurer.
- You or your spouse must be related to a sponsor who lives in any area of Australia.
- You must pass the points test (pass mark currently 110 points). You will be awarded 15 points for a relationship to your sponsor.
- You must apply to General Skilled Migration in Adelaide (see page 156).

You will need…

The following documentation is required for *all* visa applications:

- Your completed application form
- The visa application charge. Currently, the fee for most skilled visa applications is A$1,795 (around £800). Fees change often, so check before you send.
- Certified copies of official documents, such as certificates of birth, marriage and divorce. Certification is carried out by a lawyer or JP.

- Photocopies of other relevant documents, such as bank statements (for the previous three months) or employer references
- Skill assessment documentation from your occupational trade body.

With all visa applications, you will be contacted if more information is required. Generally, applications take around a year, but you will be contacted after around eight or nine months and asked to go ahead with police and health checks.

Police checks

You need to apply for a police clearance certificate. For details look for form 47P on the DIMIA websites (see page 156). Anyone with a substantial police record will be refused a visa. Even if you have spent convictions, do declare them on your application. Failure to disclose information could lead to a visa being cancelled. When dealing with bureaucrats, honesty really is the best policy.

Health checks

All applicants must have a medical examination. Those over the age of 11 will need a chest x-ray, and those over 15 an HIV test. The Australian High Commission will give you details of forms and medics authorized to carry out the tests. You will have to pay for the examinations. The only illness that automatically makes you ineligible for a visa is tuberculosis. Other conditions, including HIV and AIDS, will be considered on an individual basis.

Family Migration Stream

To qualify for a visa in this division, you must be sponsored by a family member in Australia. There are four categories:

1. Partner Migration Visa (either a spouse, fiancé(e) or same-sex partner – Australia is refreshingly liberated when it comes to gay and lesbian couples)
2. Child Migration Visa
3. Parent Migration Visa
4. Other visa (such as aged dependent relative)

For more information on these types of visa go to the DIMIA website (see page 156). When you are ready to lodge your application, send it to the Migration Branch of the Australian High

Commission (see page 156). Do not enclose your passport. You will receive a letter within 28 days acknowledging that your application has been received. Contact the Commission only if you haven't received an acknowledgement after that time. You will be contacted when your application has been decided. In the meantime, *do not* call for a bulletin. Staff do not take kindly to people ringing up to find out how their application is going.

Other visa options

There are several other types of visa that may be relevant to your circumstances, but generally these aren't so popular with migrating Brits.

Business Skills Visa

This is designed to help successful business people set up businesses in Australia and is dealt with in two stages. Successful migrants are granted a Business Skills (Provisional) Visa for four years. They can then apply for a Business Skills (Residence) Visa after establishing their business in Australia if they meet certain requirements laid down by the immigration department. There are four categories of Business Skills Visas:

1. Business owner
2. Senior executive
3. Investor
4. Business talent (a one-stage visa for outstanding business migrants sponsored by a state or territory government).

All applications for a Business Skills (Provisional) Visa and a Business Talent Visa should be sent to the Perth Business Skills Processing Centre (PBSPC, see page 156). Applications are valid only if lodged at this centre.

Employer Sponsored Visa

You may apply for this type of visa if an employer sponsors you to fill a job vacancy. There are four channels through which migrants can apply:

1. Employer Nomination Scheme – this allows employers in Australia to recruit staff from abroad if they cannot fill their vacancy through the national labour market.
2. Regional Sponsored Migration Scheme – for employers in regional or low population growth areas who cannot fill their posts nationally.
3. Labour Agreements – these allow Australian employers to recruit several overseas workers.
4. Invest Australia Support Skills – these encourage international businesses to set up in Australia.

All Employer Sponsored Visa applications must be lodged with the Migration Branch of the Australian High Commission in London (see page 156).

So you've finally done it. Nice one, cobber! All that work, waiting and praying have finally paid off. Here's what happens next.

You'll be issued with a five-year visa that lets you travel in and out of Australia several times. After that you must apply for a resident's return visa for trips abroad. If you are granted Australian citizenship, you do not need a visa to re-enter Australia.

Citizenship

To apply for citizenship you must have lived in Australia as a permanent resident for two out of the last five years. You can apply online, by post or in person at any DIMIA office in Australia or the UK (see page 156). The application takes around three months and involves a short interview and yet more form-filling.

Martin Dilkes, believes that employing a migration agency is the best way to go:

'Here is only one tip I'd give to people moving to Australia – employ a migration agency to sort out your visas! Ours did everything for us and were wonderful. It's worth every single penny. You've got enough to sort out without worrying about visas and points systems and selection processes as well. And applying for a visa is expensive. A good agency will tell you straight away if you aren't going to get through, saving you a fortune. And they'll make sure you apply for the right sort of visa. If you go for the wrong one and get turned down it's not only expensive, but your dreams will go up in smoke as well.

Pets

Australia's quarantine laws are extremely strict and complex. You need to apply for a permit to import your pet. Forms for this can be downloaded from the Australian government's Department of Agriculture, Fisheries and Forestry (AFF) website (see page 156).

When you arrive in Oz your pet will have to spend 30 days at one of the country's three quarantine stations in Sydney, Melbourne or Perth. When you book your pet on to a flight, the airline will notify one of the stations of your pet's import permit number and when it will arrive. Your pet will be met by an Australian Quarantine and Inspection Service officer, who will take it through customs and then to the quarantine station. You can visit your pet throughout its quarantine.

Fees

You can expect to pay the following fees for cats and dogs.

- Quarantine entry – A$14
- Vet inspection – usually A$71
- Document clearance – usually A$35.50
- Transport to quarantine station – A$95 between 8 a.m. and 4 p.m., otherwise A$120
- Cat accommodation – A$12 per day for the first cat, A$9 per day for others
- Dog accommodation – A$16 per day for the first dog, A$11 per day for others

Fees vary for other animals. For more details go to the AFF website (see page 156).

Your car

Most people find that it is simply too expensive to take their car with them to Australia. It is much cheaper to sell your car in the UK and buy a new one when you get there. But if your car's very dear to you, you can contact a specialist removal firm for details.

Other belongings

You can take most personal items and household goods, including furniture, into Australia tax and duty free provided they are your personal property and not for sale once you are there. You will need a detailed inventory of all your possessions and an estimated value for each item.

Food, plants and anything made from animal or plant products, such as wooden furniture and Christmas decorations made from pine cones, must be declared at customs for quarantine checks. This is to prevent pests and diseases from being taken into Australia. Any objects showing evidence of infestation may need to be treated, and you will be charged for the cost of the treatment. Put all the items of possible concern in the same container(s).

If you take foreign cash into Australia, you must declare it at customs.

The electricity supply is 240/250 volts AC, which means that your electrical equipment will work once you've changed the plugs.

Get a Home

Most Aussies live in towns and cities on the east and south coasts. Lucky them! The major centres have all the shops and cafés any dedicated shopaholic or foodie could dream of. But Australians are also good at green. Towns and cities are laced with parks and gardens. And then there are the beaches. What better way of winding down after a hard day at the office than a long dip in the warm ocean?

Sounds like paradise? Well, it just gets better. Although prices vary enormously according to area, on the whole, both buying and renting are cheaper than in the UK. Australia is a nation obsessed with buying and doing up houses. There are beautifully renovated Victorian properties for sale, but Aussies also do modern, and many newly built homes are stunning.

But a word of warning. Don't get carried away in the rush to land your dream home. Do not sign any contract to buy, rent or build until you fully understand every word. Contracts are legally binding once you have signed. As in the UK, get expert legal advice if you are planning to buy or build a home. Consult the *Yellow Pages* to find details of solicitors and check that the one you choose is registered with the Australian Law Society.

Renting

It's wise to set up a rental before you leave the UK, and in our experience, it's quite straightforward. Various websites give details of properties to rent listed according to area (see page 156).

To rent a property you will need…
- A refundable deposit
- Several weeks' rent in advance
- Two references

Make sure you get a receipt immediately for any money you hand over. While the vast majority of landlords are perfectly honest, you don't want to find yourself in a situation where you're constantly told that your receipt is 'in the post'.

Most rental houses are unfurnished, but you can usually expect a fitted kitchen with some appliances and built-in wardrobes in bedrooms. You, however, will have to provide furniture.

Flats are usually called 'units', and in some coastal areas they're let only on a short-term (holiday) basis, which can make finding a suitable base for your first few months a bit difficult. It might be an idea to search a bit further inland if you're having no luck finding anywhere to rent right on the coast.

Look out for properties with solar-heated water – your hot water will be free. In summer, all houses in Australia need some form of cooling – ceiling fans, air-conditioning or, best of all, a pool. During the winter you will occasionally need some form of heating. Be careful as some rental properties won't have any form of heating, and it's not always the first thing you think of when looking around a potential new home in a sun-soaked country. If you do have to provide your own, take account of the fact that portable gas and electric heaters are pretty expensive to run.

Rental contracts

Your lease, called an Agreement for Tenancy, will normally be for a minimum of six months. Make sure you read it carefully or get advice before signing; you can't take for granted that the terms and conditions will be the same as in the UK. In Australia, terms and conditions vary from state to state. For example, landlords are usually required to give you 21 days' notice to quit, but this is not always the case. In most states the Office of Fair Trading publishes a guide to renting; look in the phone book for details of your nearest office.

Utilities

Tenants pay for services, such as electricity, gas and telephone. Landlords usually pay the water charges, unless the property you rent has a water meter, in which case you may be required to pay for any water you use over a specified amount.

Insurance

Your landlord is usually responsible for rates and buildings insurance, but you must get contents insurance. Make sure the contract clearly states who is responsible for what before you sign.

Fees

You will normally have to pay a week or two's rent for the agent's fee, as well as paying a deposit (normally about one month's rent), which is returnable at the end of the tenancy so long as there are no outstanding bills or damage.

Buying

Any permanent resident or citizen can buy property. However, temporary residents must apply for approval from the Foreign Investment Review Board (see page 156).

Of course, it isn't wise to buy a property in Oz from the UK, but you can research prices and get an idea of what's available before you go by checking out property websites (see page 156) and the property sections of Australian newspapers .

Once you're in Australia, look at the real-estate sections in local newspapers and pick up the free catalogues distributed by real-estate agents. Note that estate agents should be registered with the Real Estate Institute in the state in which they operate.

Many homes are sold at auction in Australia, so if you go down this route but have no experience of the process, we'd really recommend you go along to a few auctions first to see how they work. This can help to steady your nerves when you do it for real, which in turn can help you stay within your budget.

In July 2000 the government introduced the First Home Owner Grant. This is a one-off payment of A$7,000 that Australian citizens or permanent residents (immigrants who have lived in Australia for more than two years) who are buying or building their first home may be eligible for. Visit the website for further details (see page 156).

Signing on the dotted line

It might be stating the obvious, but always get a solicitor to inspect any paperwork before you sign it. The process of buying property varies from state to state, but here's a general guide to help you along.

When you find the perfect house, contact the estate agent, who will provide a document disclosing information about the property. This is usually called a draft contract and includes details such as the name of the registered owner of the property, the dimensions of the land, what is included in the sale, such as outbuildings, curtains and carpets, the results of legal searches on the property and what kind of title (Good or Strata) applies to it.

'Good title' is the most common type of title in Australia, which ensures that when you have bought the property, no one will pop out of the woodwork and claim it is theirs.

'Strata title' applies to flats and units, and covers the property, its parking space (if applicable) and any easements. (Easements detail restrictions on how you can modify a property, specifying, for example, that you have to ensure right of way across the land.)

Then it's up to you to make an offer. If it's accepted, you will sign a contract of sale, which includes the information in the draft contract plus your own details and the agreed price. Ensure that the contract is subject to the outcome of building and pest inspections on the property.

On signing, you will pay a deposit to the selling agent, usually about 10% of the asking price. This is generally placed in a trust account and any interest made is shared between the seller and the purchaser when the sale is finalized. Make sure you receive a trust account receipt.

There is usually a five-business-day cooling-off period. Most people use this time to arrange building and pest inspections, which the buyer pays for. If you decide to pull out during the cooling-off period, you must pay 0.25% of the purchase price to the seller.

If you pull out after the cooling-off period, you will lose your deposit. If unexpected problems with the property surface after the exchange of contracts, the contract can usually be cancelled before settlement. Before you sign the contract, you and your solicitor should examine it thoroughly. Sometimes the cooling-off period is waived, usually if it looks as though another buyer is interested in the same property and is ready to exchange contracts straight away. The property becomes yours at settlement, usually six to eight weeks after contracts are exchanged.

You will be required to pay Stamp Duty, currently about 10% of the property's value, when you buy.

Gazumping
As in the UK, gazumping is alarmingly common in Australia. Beware if an estate agent asks you for a holding deposit – legally it means nothing. Until contracts are exchanged, there is no obligation to sell to you, and gazumping can occur.

Buying at auction
If you buy a property at an auction, you will need to pay a deposit (usually 10%) immediately after the auction. The estate agency will put the money into a trust fund until the purchase is complete. You, or a representative, will also have to sign the contract on the spot.

After an auction, there is no cooling-off period in which to change your mind or make any alterations to the contract, so make sure you have all building and pest inspections carried out before the auction. If you pull out, you will lose your deposit.

Building a home
Many Australians build their own homes. If you wish to do the same, discuss your plans with an architect registered with the

Royal Australian Institute of Architects (see page 156). A word of warning: use only licensed contractors to carry out the work. This will ensure that everything is done to a decent standard. Rules and regulations governing the licensing of contractors in Australia are drawn up on a state rather than a national basis, so your first port of call should be the local planning office (or equivalent). Should something go wrong, legal redress is also determined by state authorities, so it's vital that you check your rights before you even buy your plot of land. After all, you want to go into this with your eyes open.

Property taxes

In Australia property taxes are called council rates, and work like council tax in the UK. The money levied goes towards paying for local services, such as road maintenance, libraries and refuse collection.

Rates are calculated as a percentage of a property's rateable value, and the amount varies considerably between states. Check what you're letting yourself in for before you buy or rent.

Land tax is also levied in all states except the Northern Territory, but you pay only if your land is over a certain value. Again, the amount varies considerably between states, so check before you make a commitment.

Mortgages

Banks, credit unions and building societies can all lend you the money to buy your home. The principal lenders are the Commonwealth Bank and Westpac. Banks are the most widely used lenders, accounting for over 80% of the market.

There are also many mortgage brokers and home loan companies in the finance market. Search the net for companies.

How large a mortgage can I get?
Most experts agree that mortgage payments should be up to 30% of your monthly income, although this isn't set by law, and many people do have a larger mortgage.

How is income calculated?
You can have your income calculated on one person's earnings, or combined earnings.

What if I'm not employed?
It is unlikely you'll be given a mortgage in Australia unless you can prove you have a regular income.

Are there any charges?
You may have to pay the following fees:
- Some but not all lenders charge an application fee (anything up to A$850).
- Loan registration fee, which varies from state to state.
- Stamp duty (around 0.5%) has to be paid everywhere except in the Australian Capital Territory and the Northern Territory.

What types of mortgage are available?
Endowment mortgages are not common in Australia, but are available. Most people choose a repayment mortgage, which may have a fixed or variable rate.

Connecting utilities
Electricity is supplied by local companies, such as Energy Australia. You can find details in the phone book. Contact your local company to have your supply reconnected or to put your name on the account and have your meter read. This will require filling in a form. If you are having your electricity reconnected, there is usually a charge. Bills arrive quarterly and can be paid at most banks and post offices, over the phone with your credit card, or by post.

Gas is supplied by private companies in most states; Australian Gas Ltd is one of the largest. Contact your local company (consult the phone book) for details about reconnection or getting the account transferred. Mains gas is available in all big cities, but in rural areas gas bottles are widely used. Bills are sent out quarterly and can be paid in the same way as electricity bills.

Water companies are locally run, so consult the phone book for details. In most Australian towns and cities water is scarce, so it is usually metered. However, there is still a fixed rate in some rural areas. Bills are sent out either twice yearly or quarterly, and can be paid in instalments in the same way as electricity bills.

There are lots of private companies in the **telephone** market so shop around for the best deal. To have a phone reconnected or installed, call Telstra (see the phone book). Note that if you live in the middle of nowhere, phone connections can take several weeks. Bills arrive either quarterly or every two months. You can pay at post offices, by post, by phone or at Telstra shops.

Many utilities can be paid over the phone or online under the B-pay system. Ask at your bank for more details.

TV licence

A television licence is not required in Australia.

Note: Don't bother taking your British TV and video Down Under; they use different frequencies from the Australian system, so they won't work.

Get a Job

To work in Australia you need to be an Australian citizen, an Australian permanent resident, or have a temporary visa that specifically states you are allowed to work.

There is relatively low unemployment in Australia at the moment, with many employers crying out for skilled workers, especially in jobs on the Skilled Occupation List. As in all capitalist countries, the service sector now far outweighs traditional industries and manufacturing.

In general, prices are lower in Australia, but so are wages. As a very rough guide, you need to earn the equivalent of approximately 60% of a London wage to have the same lifestyle in Sydney.

Before you go

- Research job availability online at the government's employment website and in the job sections of Australian papers (see page 157).
- Get your qualifications recognized by a trade body in the UK before you leave. Many professions operate a reciprocal agreement between Australia and the UK, so qualifications are automatically recognized. Contact your trade association for details and allow plenty of time for going through the process of recognition as it can take several months.
- Prepare a CV and keep it brief (two pages maximum).

Once you arrive

A priority when you arrive in Australia is to register at your local tax office. You will be given a Tax File Number (TFN), the Australian equivalent of a National Insurance number, which allows your tax rate to be calculated when you start work. You should also enrol with Centrelink, the government agency that pays social security and provides other forms of assistance. You won't be eligible for social security immediately, but you may be able to access some of their other services and get access to certain courses.

You can continue your job-hunting in several different ways.

Newspapers and specialist magazines are full of job ads. The best national daily newspapers are the *Australian* and the *Australian Financial Review*. Don't forget to check out local papers, such as the *Sydney Morning Herald* and the *Herald-Sun* in Melbourne.

Employment agencies can be found in all the big cities. To register with one, you will need to take your passport, your visa showing that you are entitled to work and an up-to-date CV.

Internet sites run by recruitment and temping agencies are many and various. (Use the Australian version of Google to help you find them.)

Employment contracts

In Australia working conditions and wages are governed by law, and you will be covered in one of the following ways:

Federal or State Industrial Award – a legally binding document that sets out wages, overtime, working hours, protection from unfair dismissal or unlawful termination, and leave entitlements.

Certified Agreement – an agreement between an employer and a group of employees or their union setting out, among other things, working conditions, wages and entitlements.

Australian Workplace Agreement – an individual agreement negotiated between an employee and his or her employer.

Common Law Employment Contract – a document for those such as temps, who get work through an agency, and are not covered by an award or an agreement.

Always read a contract before you sign it, and, if necessary, take expert advice.

Working hours vary enormously, with Australians working an average of around forty hours a week. Workers paid by the hour should receive overtime for any hours worked above the employment conditions set out in their contracts. Overtime tends to be paid at normal pay plus half, or double-pay for Sundays and public holidays. However, as in the UK, many professionals work extra hours for no extra pay.

There is no universally agreed minimum wage in Australia. The system under which it is set is called the Australian Workplace Agreement (AWA), which sets a minimum wage for each occupation.

You should be paid for public holidays, annual leave and sick leave, unless you are a contract or casual worker, in which case you will be paid for the hours you have worked. Australian workers in permanent positions are entitled to a minimum of four weeks' annual holiday.

Get Healthy

Australia's public health care system is called Medicare, and it is essential that you enrol. It entitles you to free treatment at any public hospital and free or subsidized treatment by doctors, dentists, opticians and suchlike. You need to be an Australian citizen or permanent resident to be eligible. You should enrol 7–10 days after your arrival in Australia by going to any Medicare office (look in your local phone book for details).

You will need…
- Proof you are an Australian resident
- Details of your address
- Details of your income and assets

Most wage-earners pay a Medicare levy, currently 1.5% of earnings. This levy is compulsory and automatically deducted from earnings, unless you fall into one of the following categories:

- You are a pensioner.
- You are a war veteran or a war veteran's widow.
- You are a single person earning less than A$13,807 per year.

Single parents and couples with children with incomes of below A$28,200 pay a smaller Medicare levy. For further information, check out the government's health websites (see page 000). We advise you take out travel insurance that includes health cover for the first month after you leave the UK just to make sure you're covered for all health eventualities.

GPs

As a Medicare patient, you will be treated free at any surgery that advertises itself as a Bulk Billing Practice. (This means that the practice bills Medicare direct for your treatment.) If you go to a non-Bulk Billing Practice, you can claim back all or some of the fee. Non-Medicare patients have to pay to see a doctor. You can choose your own GP and if you're not happy with your choice, it's quite easy to change.

Private health care

While private health care is tax-deductible, do check carefully what you must pay for a private scheme. The public health system is so good that you might find you don't need private health cover. If you decide you do want

the added peace of mind of a private scheme, there are two main types:

Ancillary cover pays for private dentists, opticians and other health practitioners.
Hospital cover pays towards the cost of private hospital treatment. The percentage paid depends on the premium you pay.

Hospitals

Dial 000 for an ambulance, or go to the emergency department of your local public hospital. It's worth remembering that Medicare doesn't cover the cost of ambulances, but it does cover all the costs for Medicare patients in public hospitals.

Pharmacies

Pharmacies, indicated by a green or red cross, are open during normal shopping hours. Details of the nearest 24-hour pharmacy will be displayed on the door.

Centrelink (the social security service) provides low earners with Health Care Cards, entitling them to free prescriptions. Everyone else has to pay.

Get Wealthy

This section fills you in on handling your finances in Australia, covering everything from banks and bills to taxes and wills.

Banks

Australia has a wide range of high-street banks, the largest of which is the Commonwealth Bank of Australia. You will also see National Australia Bank, Westpac and ANZ Bank, as well as several regional banks.

Opening a bank account

It is advisable to open a bank account within six weeks of arriving in Australia, as it will really help to make setting up the rest of your new life a lot easier.

You will need…

- Passport
- Visa
- Proof of address, such as a utility bill or a lease on your new home
- Tax File Number

If you open an account after six weeks, you will probably be asked for additional forms of ID. Credit cards are commonly used, as are EFTPOS (Electronic Funds Transfer at Point of Sale) cards, both issued by banks. EFTPOS is similar to Switch/Delta, except that funds are taken from your account almost immediately. You can withdraw cash at machines using your EFTPOS card. You can also get cash back when using your card to pay for goods in shops.

Cheques

Australian banks don't issue cheque guarantee cards, so you can't pay by cheque in most shops. Most people use cash or credit cards for transactions.

Withdrawing cash

Much the same as in the UK, you can withdraw cash by making a cheque out to yourself in the bank, or using a cash card at a machine.

Bank charges and statements

Australian banks make charges and issue statements in much the same way as UK banks.

Banking hours

Banks are open Monday to Thursday, 9.30 a.m. to 4 p.m. and Friday, 9.30 a.m. to 5 p.m.

Of course, 24-hour cash machines are widely available. Internet banking is also widespread; you can pay your bills online with the greatest of ease.

Taxes

Services and public amenities are excellent in Australia, but this is reflected in the heavy tax burden, especially on high earners. In the financial year 2003–4 tax payable for the highest incomes (over A$62,501) is 47%.

Most people are taxed under the Pay As You Go (PAYG) system, where tax is deducted from earnings by employers.

Australia has a tax-free threshold (like the UK's personal allowance).

The Australian tax year runs from 1 July to 30 June and, with only a few exceptions, every tax resident in receipt of any kind of income must lodge a tax return with the Australian Taxation Office (ATO) by 31 October. The ATO automatically sends a tax pack to all households in June. The pack includes your tax form, which must be completed and returned to the address stipulated.

You will then receive an account of the tax you owe and a date by which you must pay your bill. If your wage is your only source of income, your PAYG payments should cover your tax liability. You can pay in instalments if your bill is over a certain amount.

Income tax

Federal income tax in Australia is progressive, which means that the more you earn, the more you pay.

Mind-boggling but essential to know are Australia's laws about taxes for residents. An Australian resident will be taxed on income from anywhere in the world, but a non-resident is subject to tax only on income from Australia. So when you become a tax resident in Australia may be crucial. If this gives you a headache, it may well be worth employing the skills of a specialist.

Note: There isn't a capital gains tax in Australia; the profit on particular assets is subject to income tax.

Goods and services tax

Like VAT, a tax of 10% is included in the price you pay for most goods and services. Some items, such as basic foodstuffs, are exempt.

Land tax

Except in the Northern Territory, land tax is payable on all land over a certain value. The amount of tax levied is decided by the state or territory authorities. In many states principal residences are exempt from land tax.

Social security

Centrelink is the government agency that deals with social security, which is paid for through general taxation.

Pensions

For tax purposes, we recommend that you consider transferring your pension to Australia within six months of becoming resident (usually when you move). After this period a pension transferred from abroad will be taxed. Always consult an expert to find out what is best for you.

With a few exceptions, employers are required to make superannuation (pension) contributions for their employees, and most employees have to join a superannuation fund. Employers usually have to pay 9% of your earnings into the superannuation fund. You can also put extra money into it yourself

Wills

Laws on wills vary from state to state. For more information visit the website listed on page 157. Most experts recommend that you get an Australian will made to replace your British one when you move to Oz, and, as with all legal matters, it's always worth seeking professional advice.

Get Wise

Education in Australia is compulsory from ages six to fifteen, but most pupils go on to complete their Year 10 qualification, usually at sixteen The state provides free education for all children aged four to eighteen, but most schools have a small voluntary annual fee to cover extra activities.

Many schools require students to wear a uniform, and parents may also have to buy books and pay for outings.

To choose a school visit the website of the Commonwealth Department of Education, Training and Youth Affairs, which has links to schools in your chosen area (see page 156).

State education is of a very high standard, but there is also an extensive selection of private schools, most of which are either administered by the Catholic Education Office or by their own board. Many are single-sex and receive a subsidy from federal and state governments. Each state has its own association of private schools, which is accessible online (see page 156).

Australia's education system

Here's a quick rundown of what you can expect to encounter when you dip a toe into Australia's education system.

Pre-school, ages 3 to 6

Although not compulsory, pre-school is very popular, so register as early as possible to secure a place. Pre-school attendance is part-time and you will have to choose between a morning or an afternoon session.

Primary school, ages 5–6 to 11–12

Most children go to primary school when they are five. The first year, often called the introductory year, is like a reception class in Britain, where children don't do a lot of formal learning; they just get into the swing of school life. Learning starts in earnest in the second year of primary school.

Secondary school, ages 12–13 to 16–18

Most secondary schools in Australia are comprehensive, although in some places there are grammar schools for gifted pupils.

Children are allowed an element of choice in their studies at secondary school, but English, maths and science are compulsory. In the last two years they specialize in subjects that will be beneficial for work or university, and are awarded an overall grade before they leave. While states and territories set their own exams, the most common exams are the School Certificate for 16-year-olds, and the Higher School Certificate for 18-year-olds.

School year

In general, the Australian school year is split into four terms: end of January to mid-April; end of April to beginning of July; mid-July to end of September; mid-October to mid-December. There are two-week breaks between terms, except for the summer holiday, which lasts for about six weeks.

School hours are around 9.00 a.m. to 3.00 p.m. with a one-hour break for lunch.

Get Around

On the road

The National Highway system, a network of well-maintained roads, links all Australia's big cities. While some highways are free, others charge tolls, usually between A$2 and A$3. Not surprisingly, Australian drivers aren't happy about paying tolls, so the roads that charge them are usually quiet.

Roads in cities tend to get clogged with

traffic, so many urbanites walk or cycle, or get public transport to work instead.

In the back of beyond, roads are sometimes little more than dirt tracks, so proceed with care.

Road laws are generally set by state governments and vary from state to state.

On arrival in Australia, you are entitled to drive on your UK licence for three months. Within this time you must apply for an Australian licence. You will normally have to undergo practical and theory tests, and an eyesight assessment.

Driving Tips

- Australians drive on the left.
- Seat-belts are compulsory for all passengers.
- Special car seats and restraints are compulsory for children up to 26 kg.
- Speed cameras are widespread and drink-driving laws strictly enforced.
- Minimum driving ages vary from state to state, but range from 16 to 18.
- Speed limits are 60 km/h in rural areas, and 100–110 km/h on highways.
- Some cities, such as Melbourne, also have a lower speed limit of 50 km/h for suburban areas.
- Registering your car is compulsory. As in the UK, you pay an annual registration fee (road tax). Where you pay, how much (usually in the region of A$300), and what documentation you need varies from state to state. For information about registering in your chosen state, see page 156.
- When driving in the country, remember to watch out for kangaroos!

Insurance

You are required by law to have at least third party insurance. Most firms operate a no-claims discount, which increases for every year without a claim up to a maximum discount of about 60%.

Australians are generally safe and careful drivers, but if the worst happens and you do have an accident, remember that you are required by law to stop, and that you have to inform the police if:

- Someone is injured
- The damage looks to be more than A$500
- The other driver appears to be under the influence of alcohol or drugs
- Any vehicle has to be towed away.

Trains

The railways are state-run, overseen by Rail Australia. City services are generally excellent with modern trains, but long-distance services can be slow – great if you want to see the countryside, but infuriating if you're in a hurry. Not surprisingly, services become less slick in remote areas.

You can buy tickets from railway stations, of course, but some city newsagents also sell tickets. You can also book online (see page 157), but this must be done at least seven days in advance.

Discounted tickets and travel cards are available for most routes, so do your homework to get the best deal.

Buses

There is an excellent bus network all over Australia, which gives better coverage than the railways. Tickets are cheap too, so the system is well worth investigating.

In cities, you can get tickets from bus stations and certain newsagents, or you can pay the driver when you get on. You have to stamp your ticket in the machine near the driver's seat. In most cities, a zoning system is in operation, which allows you to travel anywhere in a particular zone for a standard fare. Note that zone tickets are usually valid for two hours only, so check before you buy.

Travelling longer distances by bus is much cheaper than flying. The biggest long-distance bus company in Australia is Greyhound Pioneer Australia. As with trains, discounts are available, so shop around between companies.

Internal flights

Australia's two domestic airlines are Qantas and Ansett Australia, which offer regular flights between towns and cities. Richard Branson's Virgin Blue has recently entered the market, so competition is fierce. As with the cheap flights industry in the UK, you can get some good discounts if you do your homework.

Get a Life

Some 90% of Australians live near the coast, and the country's enviable climate means that outdoor pursuits are a way of life. The beach, barbies and the legendary Aussie passion for sport are all central to living Down Under.

However, the outdoor life has a price that nobody envies, namely, one of the world's worst records for skin cancer. Pale complexions from northern Europe are particularly vulnerable, so when out and about it is essential to use at least factor 30 sunscreen and to cover up whenever possible. Cancer Council Australia's website (see page 156) is a mine of valuable information. Its 'slipslopslap' campaign (slip on a shirt, slop on sunscreen, slap on a hat) is a national institution, and any child who can talk can sing you the campaign song. The council sells, among other things, dirt-cheap sun lotion plus shorts, t-shirts and swimming costumes made out of fabric that UV rays can't penetrate. You can pick them up at any pharmacy, department store or supermarket, or at the council's own shops.

Making friends

Meeting locals is easy – just go to the pub or the beach, where everyone hangs out. Australians are chatty, friendly and laid-back. Although some advertisements reinforce the popular image of Australian men as beer-swilling, sexist he-men, in reality, Australians are proud of their tolerant society, which embraces different races, religions and sexuality – in fact, everyone. So if you aren't the most PC of people, best keep it to yourself.

Steps to Social Success

- Australians are famously laid back, so you'd have to try really hard to commit a real faux pas. Observe the usual rules of good manners and you shouldn't come to any harm.
- Australians are also famously frank, so don't expect to be treated with kid gloves. Don't get upset – straight talking isn't an insult. Australians just have a tendency to tell it how it is.
- If you don't like sport, pretend you do, or learn fast. Sport, particularly cricket and rugby, is a national obsession in Australia.
- For goodness' sake, don't whinge. You don't want to support a stereotype, do you?

Expats

It is estimated that at least 9,000 Brits set up home in Australia every year, so you should be able to find some British friends, no matter where you live in Oz. You might even end up reminiscing fondly about rain and traffic jams, although somehow we doubt it. If you do have difficulty finding other expats, your first port of call should be the British Consulate; they will be able to give you details of local expat clubs.

Shopping

Australia has many huge, out-of-town shopping malls, and Australians think nothing of driving long distances to get to them. Local shops tend to be concentrated on a main road and include the usual convenience store, pharmacy, newsagent and bottle shop.

If you fancy splashing your cash, opals are good value, as Australia produces 95% of the world's supply. Diamonds and gold are also mined in Oz, so are equally good buys. Thanks to its fondness for the outdoor life, Australia produces great outdoor clothing under brand names such as Ripcurl and Billabong. And let's face it – where else in the world can you get a genuine boomerang?

Markets selling a wide range of fresh food are popular everywhere in Australia, as are craft and flea markets in cities.

Opening hours

Most shops are open Monday to Saturday, 9 a.m. to 5 p.m. Late opening is on Thursday or Friday evening. Most markets are open a couple of days a week in small towns, but may open Monday to Saturday, or even seven days a week, in cities.

Eating out

Boy, do Aussies know how to enjoy themselves! They love eating out, and there are masses of good restaurants to choose from. Australia has no national cuisine, but recent years have seen the growth of a new phenomenon – 'contemporary Australian' cuisine – a fusion of fresh ingredients inspired by its multicultural population. Indian, Greek, Italian and French jostle alongside Vietnamese, Thai, Chinese and Malaysian and often intermingle to produce dishes that surprise and delight.

Tipping is much the same as in the UK: 10% is the norm for good service in restaurants,

and a couple of dollars is welcomed by taxi drivers, porters and bar staff.

Drinking

Aussies are legendary drinkers, and most enjoy a drink or three. Friday and Saturday nights are when Australians really go for it. Most people drink in hotel bars, open from 11 a.m. to 11 p.m.

Smoking

Smoking is banned in public buildings (including pubs and restaurants), on public transport and in taxis, so it's not uncommon to see groups of people standing outside offices or pubs having a smoke.

Staying in touch

The postal service, Australian Post (AP), is cheap, quick and efficient provided you use the four-digit postcode with the address. If you don't have a settled address or you live in a remote area, you can have mail sent to a post office. Domestic post must be collected within two weeks, overseas post within four weeks.

Australia has several major telephone companies, including Telstra and Optus. Local calls cost 40 cents from public payphones and are not timed, so you can talk as long as you like. Payphones take Australian coins, and many also accept phone and credit cards.

To telephone Australia from the UK dial 00 61 and omit the first zero of the Australian number.
To telephone the UK from Australia dial 00 11 44 and omit the first zero of the UK number.

Emergencies

In an emergency dial 000 for the police, fire brigade or ambulance service.

8

New Zealand

At 1,600 kilometres beyond Australia, New Zealand is the most remote inhabited landmass on Earth. But despite being so far away, it can feel an awful lot like home. Things generally work in a familiar way. They even drive on the left. But then there's the landscape and the space, and the Kiwi attitude that they work to live not the other way around.

It might be the size of the UK, but New Zealand has a population of just 4 million, an awful lot of sheep, and some of the most spectacular, unspoilt and diverse scenery on the planet. New Zealand is made up of two large islands – the North Island and the South Island – and a number of smaller ones, some of them hundreds of kilometres from the main landmasses. The two main islands are surprisingly different: the North Island has bubbling geysers and several large volcanoes, including the active Mount Ruapehu, while the South Island has a magnificent glacial mountain range along most of its length. Both islands boast lush forests, beautiful rivers and spectacular beaches.

Much of the national identity is tied to a sense of pride in the natural beauty of the landscape, probably the last significant area on the planet to be colonized by man. When the Maori arrived 1,200 years ago they called it *Aotearoa* – the 'land of the long white cloud'. Today the Kiwis refer to their country as 'Godzone'.

New Zealanders are relaxed, down to earth, outdoorsy, into sport in a big way and impatient of snobbery. While their geographical remoteness has contributed to this way of life, it can also be a bit of a sore point. They refer to themselves as being 'at the end of the line', but don't like it much when foreigners make the same observation.

While Maori, the Polynesian people who inhabited the islands before the British arrived in 1769, currently account for about 10% of New Zealand's population, they form a disproportionate percentage of the country's poor. However, the situation is improving and there is a growing pride in the Maori heritage, which goes far deeper than the famous war-dance known as the *haka*. After nearly 250 years, New Zealanders as a whole are finally taking pride in *Maoritanga* – the Maori way of doing things.

Politics

New Zealand became independent from the UK in 1947, but remains a member of the Commonwealth. The Queen remains the head of state, and a governor-general serves as her representative. There is a Westminster-style parliament, which has only one house (elected by proportional representation), and a prime minister as head of government.

For a country often regarded as conservative, New Zealand has had a surprisingly radical political history. In 1893 it became the first country to institute votes for women, swiftly followed by workers' pensions. During the 1920s it was the first to build a comprehensive welfare state, and in 1999 it elected the world's first transgender MP, Georgina Beyer.

Government in New Zealand reflects a national trend for women to occupy top jobs, with several high-ranking women in government, including the prime minister, Helen Clark.

Economy

In the 1940s New Zealand was the most prosperous country in the world. Things aren't quite that good today – but they're not bad either. New Zealand recently ranked third in the world, after Hong Kong and Singapore, in a league of countries with the most economic freedom. For the man or woman in the street that means a low level of taxation.

Traditionally, New Zealand is an agricultural nation. Meat (the ubiquitous lamb), dairy and wool products remain the mainstay of the country's prosperity. Forestry, fishing and tourism are also important. Unemployment and inflation are low, and while average wages are low compared to those in the UK, the cost of living is significantly cheaper.

Currency

New Zealanders use the New Zealand dollar (NZ$)

Religion

New Zealand is predominantly a Christian country, but the number of churchgoers has been declining in recent years. Some 37% of the population now describe themselves as of no religion. Of the remainder, Protestants are the largest group and make up 37%, Roman Catholics 13% and a number of religions account for the remaining 13%.

Time difference

New Zealand is 12 hours ahead of GMT. Daylight Saving Time puts the clocks forward an hour during their summer (October to March).

Climate

Being in the southern hemisphere, New Zealand has seasons the reverse of those in the north. Summer is October to March and winter is June to September.

The climate is warmer and sunnier than the UK's, but can be wet. It differs between the warmer, more tropical North Island and the cooler, more seasonal South Island, where skiing is popular during the winter. The whole of New Zealand gets its fair share of rain, but the west coasts of both islands get the worst of it.

Brits in New Zealand

Defining the British expat community in New Zealand is difficult. The shared language and cultural heritage, not to mention the head of state, mean that Kiwis and Brits have lots in common. An estimated 17% of New Zealanders are entitled to a British passport, although many more can claim British descent. Newcomers from the UK therefore tend to assimilate easily.

Love/Hate

'The space is fantastic. We came from the southeast of England and there is just no comparison. There are three times as many people living inside the M25 as in the whole of New Zealand.'

'One of the most significant differences is that New Zealanders accept you for who you are, not what you are. On my trips back to the UK I find people so pretentious.'

'I have to pinch myself, even after four years, as I drive to work with glorious views all around. Being so close to work allows me to nip back to see school plays and sports if I choose, and I really feel part of the kids' everyday lives.'

'If you are looking for lifestyle and opportunity, then New Zealand is certainly the place to consider. There are amazing opportunities for anyone who is even slightly entrepreneurial.'

'I love the people, the beauty of the country and the accessibility of great places just for the weekend. If I had wanted a really hot country, I would have gone to Australia, so the weather here suits me just fine. The air is so clear and the night sky is wondrous.'

'Both girls enjoy school and have found their peers much more friendly than in the UK. There are a lot more sports and after-school activities here. Kiwis are especially into rugby and netball.'

'The scenery is just breathtaking – rugged terrain, lush rolling hills, wide open spaces, a glistening ocean within ten minutes of home, snowcapped mountains in the distance. Also the weather is much nicer than in England.'

'Any drawbacks? It sounds obvious, but it's a hell of a long way from home…'

'A shared language might make you think there won't be any culture shocks, but there are – it just takes a bit longer for the penny to drop.'

'I miss the subtle, dry sense of humour that many English people have, and the quality of TV, radio and newspapers is abysmal here in comparison. I crave Radio Four and decent adverts on the telly.'

'The education system is quite different from the UK. I believe it's of a lower standard here. Our youngest daughter was doing maths that she had done two years ago in England. Also, I think they lack imagination with education. It's very staid.'

'Tin-roof houses were a real eye-opener. Also, most homes are one level only.'

'They don't have supermarkets like Tesco's and Sainsbury's, which I do miss.'

'I still miss the wider range of the clothes shopping, but over the years the consumer goods have come down in price and the range has expanded.'

Get There

So you want to go and live in New Zealand? That's great, but remember that New Zealand has to want you too. Like Australia, it has stringent immigration controls to keep out undesirables.

If you want to make New Zealand your promised land, you have to be prepared for a fair bit of hard work and organization before you even begin to think about packing. Your first port of call will be the New Zealand Immigration Service (NZIS). They have a comprehensive website with loads of the most recent information and forms you can download. It is by far the easiest, cheapest and most reliable way of finding out the information you need.

Failing that, you can call their premium-rate telephone helpline, or visit them in person. Opening times are given on the website. For all contact details, see page 157.

Getting your visa

It is essential to check with the NZIS for the most up-to-date information before embarking on your visa application. You must pass a points test to establish your desirability as an immigrant, and the pass mark can change from month to month. New visa categories are also introduced from time to time.

Getting a visa is not an easy process, so should you decide you need advice or someone to handle your application for you, there are plenty of people who act as immigration consultants – for a price. The New Zealand Association for Migration and Investment (NZAMI) can provide a list of immigration consultants (see page 157), but consultants are not legally obliged to be registered with NZAMI, so make sure you ask for references.

The United Kingdom has a visa waiver agreement with New Zealand, which means that UK passport holders with a return air ticket, a valid passport and proof of sufficient funds may visit New Zealand as tourists for up to six months *without* a visa. But if you wish to work, study and generally start making a new life, you will need to get an appropriate visa before you depart. You can, however, use the tourist visa to look for a job in New Zealand.

There are several categories of visa, and the average processing time in London for permanent residence visas is 4–6 months. If you already have a job offer in New Zealand, or are making an application on family grounds, the processing time could be reduced to 1–3 months.

Several recent changes have made it more, rather than less, difficult to get New Zealand residency. The six-month Job-search Visa has been eliminated, although this does not significantly affect UK subjects, as there is nothing to stop you entering the country on a tourist visa and using your six months to look for a job.

The popular General Skills Visa has been eliminated and replaced by a more stringent Skilled Migrant Visa aimed at actively recruiting people who will fill gaps in the New Zealand skills pool. If you visit the NZIS website, you will be able to access the current Skill Shortages List, and if you fit into one of the categories, it will contribute to the points you require for your visa.

Note: There are changes afoot in the business categories, so check the website carefully if this section applies to you.

You will have to pay for your visa, and it isn't cheap. Prices change regularly and vary from £45 for a Visitor's Visa to over £800 for a Long-term Business Visa. Once your visa has been approved, you will also need to pay a 'migrant levy' of about £40–£50. Cheques and a range of debit and credit cards are acceptable, but all payments must be made in sterling.

Types of visa

It is your responsibility to ensure that you are applying for the right visa to suit your circumstances. The rules change frequently, so do your research thoroughly.

Note that for almost all categories of visa, an English language standard applies. This is waived for applicants from the UK, as it is assumed they will already have a competent level of English.

New Zealand–United Kingdom Working Holiday Scheme Visa

This is open to those aged 18–30 who want to go for a working holiday in New Zealand. An annual quota of 9,000 visas is available for British applicants, and the quota is renewed annually on 1 September. Postal applications can take up to six weeks during busy periods, so if you would like to apply in person, take your current passport and the application fee of £45 to the New Zealand Immigration Service (see page 157) and they should be able to issue your visa on the spot.

Student Visa

To gain a Student Visa you must already have been accepted for a study course in New Zealand. You will need to fill in the appropriate form, produce a receipt for payment of the course fee, a guarantee of accommodation and evidence of sufficient maintenance funds.

Skilled Migrant Visa

This type of visa replaced the General Skills Visa in early 2004. At the time of writing, details were unavailable, but it is expected that the Skilled Migrant Visa will involve a two-stage process in which you are 'invited to apply' for residency once certain criteria have been met.

The new visa will be more firmly targeted at filling New Zealand's skills gaps, with bonus points awarded for job offers outside Auckland, or for qualifications and experience specific to skills shortages. Applicants with no skilled job offer, but who show the potential to settle and contribute to New Zealand, may be granted a two-year work permit as a pathway to residency.

Investor Visa

Open to anyone up to the age of 84, this type of visa requires no formal qualifications, but does require a minimum investment of NZ$1 million for at least two years. The points pass mark is set once a year, and a residence permit is issued provided certain conditions are met for two years.

Entrepreneur Visa

Open to people of any age, this type of visa requires no formal qualifications, points or funds. However, applicants must establish a business (showing a business plan) or buy a business in New Zealand that benefits the country in certain prescribed ways. You can apply for this visa if you have already established, bought or invested in (at least 25% of ownership) a business in New Zealand and have been self-employed in that business for at least two years.

Alternatively, you can apply to get into New Zealand under a Long-term Business Visa (see below), then apply for residence under the entrepreneur category in the future.

Long-term Business Visa

To qualify for a Long-term Business Visa you must be 84 or under and have a business plan and sufficient funds to invest in a business.

Work to Residence Visa

Unavailable to anyone over 55 years old, this visa requires no formal qualifications, but you may need to register any occupational qualifications you do have in New Zealand before applying.

You must work full time for two years, with a minimum salary of NZ$45,000, for an employer accredited by the NZIS, or in a job on the current Priority Occupations List.

If you happen to be an internationally recognized talent in the arts, sport or culture, special exceptions apply.

Employee of Business Relocating to New Zealand Visa

Open to people of any age, this type of visa is only for key personnel of companies relocating to New Zealand.

Family Quota Visa

To qualify for this type of visa you must have immediate family or a partner living in New Zealand. Registration, points and an English language requirement are unnecessary. Each year the government decides how many people will be allowed to enter New Zealand under the Family Quota Visa and sets new limits.

Humanitarian/Refugee Visa

Available only to refugees and their family members in critical circumstances, this type of visa has no age restrictions or English language requirement, and registration and points are unnecessary.

Points system

For certain visas, applicants are assessed and awarded points for meeting certain criteria. The pass mark is currently around 28 points, but this varies according to whether the NZIS wants to speed up or slow down rates of immigration, or perhaps just clear a backlog.

Factors assessed	Max. points awarded
Qualifications	12
New Zealand qualifications	2
Work experience, 2–20 years	10
Relevant job offer	10
(but varies according to current pass mark)	
Age	10
Settlement funds (NZ$100,000+ or NZ$200,000+)	1 or 2
Spouse's qualifications	1 or 2
Family sponsor	3

Contact the NZIS (see page 157) for more information about the points system and how to calculate your own score.

You will need...

The following documents are required for most visa applications. They are described in the order in which the NZIS likes them to be submitted.

- Covering letter stating clearly the visa you are applying for and listing the documents submitted with the application. Identify any outstanding documents that will be forwarded later. If you have a job offer, advise the immigration service of the start date so that they can prioritize the application accordingly.
- Original written job offer (if applicable) or a certified copy. The job offer should be in the form of a formal contract.
- Application form completely filled in and signed. Ensure that all family members are noted exactly as they appear on their passports, with their full dates of birth.
- Qualification certificates. If not in English, include a translation plus the certificate in the original language. If the institution and qualification are not on the List of Recognized Qualifications (see NZIS website), a Qualification Assessment

Report is needed from the New Zealand Qualifications Authority (see page 157).

- Proof of work experience (if needed for your type of visa). This can include references from previous employers, payslips and tax records. If you are self-employed, a letter from your accountant is essential. Also send other evidence, such as company registration details, tax statements and end-of-year financial reports.
- Proof of spouse's qualifications and certified copies of passport. Both can be certified by a lawyer, solicitor or justice of the peace. If not in English, provide a translation plus the certificate in the original language.
- Residence Sponsorship Form filled in and signed by your sponsor. A person authorized to take statutory declarations, such as a JP, lawyer or a public notary, must witness the declaration. The form must be accompanied by a full birth certificate of the sponsor (plus evidence of name change, if applicable) and evidence that he or she has been resident in New Zealand for at least three years.
- Evidence of settlement funds. This must show the source that the transferred funds will come from, such as bank statements, property/mortgage and estate agent evaluation, or share information.
- Full birth certificates are required for all applicants, as are marriage certificates, where applicable.
- Certified copies of passports for each applicant (certified by a lawyer, solicitor or justice of the peace).
- Divorce papers and any custodial information, if applicable. If children from a previous relationship are included in the application, you must submit legal documents stating that the parent is permitted to take them out of their home country, and supply evidence of full custody.
- English language requirement (unnecessary for British citizens resident in the UK).
- All applicants aged 17 or over must provide a police certificate from their country of citizenship and other countries where they have lived for 12 months or more in the last ten years. These reports must be no more than six months old. UK citizens can obtain them from Scotland Yard.
- Full medical report completed by a NZIS panel doctor. All applicants must produce evidence of a medical taken less than three months before the application is lodged. If you have a medical condition, you should supply a report from the specialist or GP who treated you, detailing your present condition, treatment and expected prognosis.

Filling in Forms

It is essential that forms are filled in neatly and accurately. Like it or not, bureaucrats are more likely to look favourably on a legible, well-organized application with no spelling mistakes than one that looks as though it's been hastily cobbled together down the pub.

- Do not put documents in plastic folders.
- If sending originals, enclose a photocopy.
- Do not enclose any payment with your application. It will be requested when your application is approved in principle.
- Make sure all your documentation falls within the time limits, e.g. health certificates must be less than three months old.

Citizenship

To be eligible for New Zealand citizenship you have to be either married to a New Zealand citizen or have been a permanent resident in New Zealand for more than three years.

Lots of information about applying for citizenship is available on the New Zealand government's Department of Internal Affairs website (see page 157). You can download a form from this site, or apply for one by phone, in person or by writing.

It will take anything up to eight months for your application to be processed. The current fee for granting citizenship is NZ$460.

Travel plans

The most realistic way of getting to New Zealand is by air. When planning your move, it is worth bearing in mind that high season is December, January and February, while low season is May, June and July. This could help you to keep costs down. You could also find that it's cheaper to buy a return ticket than a single.

Another thing to compare is excess baggage or airfreight charges of different airlines. You might be arriving some time before the rest of your worldly goods, so plan carefully what you need to take with you for the first few weeks.

Make sure you have booked some sort of temporary accommodation for your arrival so that you have a base while looking for a more permanent home. You could be there for up to three months while you wait for your belongings to arrive.

Many companies can offer you professional assistance with every aspect of relocation (see page 157).

Pets

If you have any animal other than a dog or a cat, do not bother reading any further. Bird, hamster, gerbil, snake, rabbit … sorry, but you can't take it.

New Zealand has very strict quarantine laws, and, luckily, so do we. Fido and Ginger therefore have a far easier time of it coming from the UK than from certain other parts of the world, and will not be subjected to quarantine. They will, however, be required to have an identity chip and up-to-date certificates for certain vaccinations.

Dogs require shots for rabies, distemper, hepatitis, canine cough, leptospirosis and parvovirus. Cats require shots for rabies, panleukopenia, rhinotracheitis and calicivirus. Both cats and dogs must also have a rabies lab test at least three weeks after the vaccination and six months *before* it can be imported – so plan well ahead.

You must get an import permit for your pet, so look on the Ministry for Agriculture and Fisheries website for the latest information (see page 157).

Although airlines classify animals as cargo, they do in fact travel in pressurized, climate-controlled sections of the hold and will be well looked after. Make sure you check which airlines are currently transporting pets, as the situation can change. Note that all imported animals must go through Auckland International Airport.

Your car

Don't even think about taking your car to New Zealand. The cost of shipping it and then getting it modified to meet the country's strict motoring standards will probably be more than it's worth. So sell your car and when you get to New Zealand you can use the cash to make the most of some of the cheapest new and used car prices in the world.

If your car is so special that you simply can't leave it behind, consult an experienced shipping firm that can help you with the customs forms.

Other belongings

If there is one piece of advice that keeps cropping up for every country in this book, it is to take as little as possible with you. Stick to the really irreplaceable or sentimental items that you cannot live without. Once you know how much you want to take, contact a removal firm that is experienced in handling moves to New Zealand. Your best bet is to log on to a search engine, such as Google, and do an advanced search on New Zealand Removals. The results pages contain many companies who will be able to help. Try to get references from the company before you hire them.

New Zealand is generally cheaper than the UK, and there are numerous second-hand shops, factory outlets and car-boot sales that will make the cost of setting up home on the other side of the world less expensive. Note that New Zealand is on a 230/240 volt 50 Hz power supply, so your electrical goods will work, but you'll need an adaptor.

As the New Zealand economy relies very heavily on farming, great care is taken that foreign agricultural diseases are not imported along with migrants. The Ministry of Agriculture and Farming and the customs authorities have the most recent lists of prohibited and restricted items, but your removal firm should also be able to give you advice.

In general, do not take gardening implements or outdoor equipment likely to be dirty unless it has been thoroughly cleaned. This includes lawnmowers, football boots, bikes and garden furniture. Plants, flowers and seeds (fresh or dried) are also out of bounds.

For customs purposes, you must compile an inventory itemizing your belongings with approximate values, and, if possible, receipts.

Get a Home

Estate agents in New Zealand employ a bewildering range of abbreviations to describe properties, which can flummox the outsider. Ever come across OPHWS? It's an Off Peak Hot Water System, of course. ROW, meanwhile, is suggestive of neighbours from hell, but actually stands for Right of Way, and ELF isn't Orlando Bloom in tights (more's the pity), but Electric Light Fitting.

The descriptions for types of housing can also take a bit of getting used to as New Zealanders have different meanings for certain UK words.

By international standards, house prices in New Zealand are extremely reasonable. The country has lots of space and a small population, which inevitably impacts on market values. However, New Zealand is currently going through a housing boom, the highest since the 1970s, so house prices and availability have been affected accordingly. Prices in many areas have increased between 50% and 300% over the last five years.

New Zealand housing standards are very stringent, and all new homes carry a 'Master Builder' certification, which is effectively a 5–10 year guarantee on quality of workmanship. Note, however, that few houses have central heating, air-conditioning or double-glazing.

Before you go

You can, of course, start house hunting on the Internet, but if you do spot the house of your dreams, it could be sold by the time you actually reach New Zealand. It might be worth setting up some appointments for your first week, but in reality, who has time to do this while packing up for the move and saying their goodbyes?

Most people leave the search for a home until they arrive, and book into temporary accommodation while they find their feet. The website for the New Zealand *Yellow Pages* lists hotels and B&Bs (see page 157). If you really can't stand the idea of living in short-term limbo, a relocation or resettlement company (see page 157) can be a real boon, as they will work with you to identify your requirements, conduct preliminary searches and review them with you before you leave the UK. They will use their local knowledge to draw up a shortlist of areas and properties to meet your requirements.

When you arrive

There are three main places to start your search for a home:

- Real-estate agents – they charge a fee on completion of the tenancy agreement or sale.
- Newspaper property sections – Wednesday and Saturday are the best days to look at these.
- Letting centres – these charge a fee for looking at their lists. They are cheaper than estate agents, but you might not find the property you want.

As in the UK, many companies have websites with property details and even web tours of the houses, see page 157.

The systems for renting and buying property in New Zealand are well regulated, and designed to be as simple as possible while safeguarding the rights of all parties.

Types Of New Zealand Housing

Flat: A room in a 'single family dwelling' where you share a 'common' kitchen and perhaps a bathroom with others.

Apartment: What we Brits would think of as a flat in a multistorey building.

Townhouse: Attached, semi-detached or detached multistorey house in a development of similar-style buildings.

Unit: A bit like a NZ townhouse; one of several adjoining homes in a residential complex.

Villa: An older property, usually wooden, in Victorian style.

Section: The plot a property is built on/garden.

Lifestyle section: Rural plot with several acres of land and a bespoke house.

Renting

Everything to do with renting a property in New Zealand, from deposits to disputes, is overseen by Tenancy Services, a department of the Ministry for Housing. Download their booklet 'Renting and You' from their website (see page 157).

Most rental property in New Zealand is unfurnished, but usually includes things such as carpets, curtains and cookers. It may not, however, include any heating.

To rent a property you will need…

- 2–4 weeks' rent as a bond (deposit) – this is refundable
- 2 weeks' rent in advance
- 1 week's rent for the agent's commission plus tax @ 12.5%
- A previous landlord's written reference is helpful, but not essential.

Rental contracts

Tenancy agreements are simple, standardized forms, and deposits (or 'bonds', as they are known in New Zealand) are administered by Tenancy Services. They will also deal with any dispute between landlord and tenant. The following rules always apply:

- There is a time limit after you have signed the agreement before the landlord can increase the rent.
- The landlord is legally obliged to give you 60 days' notice of any increase.
- The Tenancy Services website has a list of market rates for rent comparisons. If you feel you are being charged too much, you can apply to a tenancy tribunal, which will perform a market reassessment. If you are being overcharged, the landlord will be forced to reduce your rent for a stipulated period – usually six months.
- The landlord is responsible for repairs unless caused by the tenant or their guests.
- The landlord must give the tenant 24 hours' notice of repair work being carried out.
- In the first instance the landlord should be informed of the repair needed. If he cannot be contacted and the situation is urgent, the tenant may get the repair done and be reimbursed later.
- If a request for a repair is ignored, write to the landlord asking for it to be done within ten working days. If it is still not done, you can take the matter to a tenancy tribunal.

It is worth knowing that if you sign a tenancy agreement containing clauses outside the law, it cannot be enforced. For example, if you agree to 30 days' notice from the landlord, he cannot enforce it because the law states that the tenant must be given 42 or 90 days' notice, depending on circumstances.

The landlord will also supply a Bond Lodgement Form, which both he and the tenant must complete and sign. The landlord must deposit the form and the bond with Tenancy Services within 23 days. They will send a receipt to you and the landlord. The bond is fully returnable when the tenant leaves, provided no damage has been done to the property.

Tenancy Services will supply a Property Inspection Report, which is an inventory stating what condition the property is in. It will list existing damage, such as scorch marks on the carpet, so that there is no dispute when the tenant comes to leave about who caused it.

Utilities

The tenant must pay for electricity, gas and telephone connections. Water is metered in some, but not all, properties, and the tenant must pay the water charges.

Insurance

The owner is responsible for buildings insurance and rates. The tenant is responsible for contents insurance.

There are various other fairly predictable rights and responsibilities for both landlord and tenant not covered above. Find them in the booklet, 'Renting and You'.

Buying

Like renting, buying in New Zealand is a simple, well-regulated and 'gentlemanly' process not subject to the gazumping and other skullduggery we are used to in the UK. Nonetheless, you must still thoroughly research the market, and here's how to go about it.

Getting to know the Real Estate Institute of New Zealand website inside out is the best favour you can do yourself (see page 157). It has country-wide listings of properties, comparative house prices and mortgages, and lots of advice.

Real-estate agencies are the next obvious place to look, and many of them have websites. Look, too, at newspaper property sections, particularly on Wednesday and Saturday. Some of these may be accessed online (see page 157).

Private sales, which cut out the estate agent, are often made on the Internet. See page 157 for the most popular website.

The average time from initial offer to completion is 3–4 weeks. Although you are not legally obliged to use a lawyer, most people do because he or she helps you to negotiate the price, do title searches, check contracts, draw up the necessary documents, arrange for settlement, advises you of tax implications and generally safeguards your rights. Fees will be in the region of NZ$400 to NZ$600.

An estate agent or conveyancer can serve a similar role to the lawyer, but an agent can work out more expensive because the charge is based on a percentage of the property value rather than being a set fee.

1. Making an offer

Once you have found your home, the first thing to do is make a formal offer in writing. This should include a sum for chattels (fixtures and fittings) included in the sale. First offers are often conditional upon a number of factors, such as finance being approved, independent valuations, title searches, building inspection or sale of another property.

2. Agreement to purchase

When the offer has been accepted, a 10% deposit is paid to the estate agent or lawyer handling your purchase. They are legally required to hold it for ten days, or until the conditions of sale, such as the title search, are met.

3. The contract

The contract will specify the settlement date (when the property becomes legally yours, the final price is paid and you can move in)

and the terms of the sale. It takes roughly three weeks between contracts being drawn up and settlement, but this timing can vary enormously depending on lots of different factors. Once the contract is agreed, it becomes unconditional, and there are penalties if the sale does not go ahead.

Note: There is no Stamp Duty in New Zealand.

Rates

Rates are tied to the value of your house and vary by region. Rate charges cover water, recycling, sewerage, general services, rivers and transport.

Mortgages

New Zealand has a buoyant and competitive mortgage market, so do your homework and look around. Comparisons of competitive mortgages are available online.

Banks and financial services institutions are efficient, have a wide range of products to suit all circumstances, and can usually arrange a mortgage within 24 hours. The major lenders include Bank of New Zealand, Westpac Trust, National Bank, ASB Bank and Kiwi Bank.

Most mortgages are capped at 95%, and the terms and conditions will depend on your individual circumstances.

You will need...

- Proof of income, such as a letter of employment or a tenancy agreement
- Copy of the Sale and Purchase Agreement for the property (prepared by the real estate agent, this becomes legally binding when signed by both the purchaser and vendor)
- Copy of a registered independent valuation (some banks will make you use their own approved valuer)
- Proof of past credit history (bank statements are usually acceptable)

How large a mortgage can I get?

Most experts think your monthly mortgage repayments should be no more than one third of your net monthly income. You can't get a 100% motgage in New Zealand – you have to put down a deposit of at least 5%, but many banks ask for around 20%. As a result, many New Zealanders rent because they can't afford such a large deposit.

How is income calculated?

Income can be calculated on single or joint earnings.

What if I'm not employed?

As in most countries, it is unlikely you will be given a mortgage unless you can prove you have a regular monthly income.

When do I arrange a mortgage and how long will it take?

As in the UK, you arrange a mortgage when your offer on a property has been accepted, and the process takes approximately the same amount of time.

Are there any charges?

The amount you will be charged can vary enormously, depending on a number of factors, including the part of the country in which you live. Most experts agree that you should budget up to 5% of your home's value for fees, which will include the mortgage lender's administration fees, the lawyer's fees and the fee for the transfer of deeds.

Connecting utilities

As in most countries, utility companies in New Zealand are regional, so there are many different ones. Check in the phone book when you arrive and make comparisons before you sign a contract.

Note: Very few properties in New Zealand have mains gas; most households use bottled gas. Telecom New Zealand deals with telephone connections.

TV licence

You don't need a television licence in New Zealand because all the channels are completely funded by advertising. Note that it isn't worth taking your TV to New Zealand; it's cheaper to buy when you get there than pay for transportation.

Get a Job

New Zealand has a low unemployment rate, on a par with the UK's in recent years. But wages are low by international standards, and many Kiwis have relocated to Australia, where wages are higher.

Having said that, do not expect getting a job in New Zealand to be a piece of cake. First you will need a visa, which entitles you to a work permit. Once you have a work permit, employers will be happy to interview you for any position they have open. However, the new skilled migrant rules make it more than likely that your visa will be contingent on a job offer. Remember that employers are not permitted to make a job offer to anyone who is not resident in New Zealand unless the position appears on the Skill Shortages List posted on the NZIS website. (Recent shortages have been listed in telecommunications, information technology, wholesale distribution, orcharding and tourism.)

Of the two main centres of population, Auckland is home to the nation's manufacturing, service and distribution sectors, while finance, government, film, television and IT are centred in Wellington, the capital. The rest of the country is devoted mainly to farming, fishing, forestry and food processing, with pockets of industry, electronics and mining.

New Zealand prides itself on being class- and hierarchy-free. Working relations are casual, but respectful. Bosses often invite staff to their homes for a barbecue and 'Friday fives' (end of the week drinks).

If you are thinking of setting up your own business, consult the website listed on page 157 for lots of useful information.

Before you go

If possible, try to line up a job before you go to New Zealand. This will also open up the number of visa categories you can apply for.

- Research job availability online at the government's employment websites and in those compiled by newspapers and specialists (see page 157). Be ready to chase people up, as response times can be slow.
- Look at professional publications with online job listings, such as those devoted to teaching (see page 157).
- Check if you need to register your

professional or trade qualifications with the Registration Board before you can work or apply for a job. For details, visit the government websites on page 157.
- Prepare a CV and keep it brief (two pages maximum).

Once you arrive

- To start work or open a bank account you will need an IRD number from the Inland Revenue Department (see page 157) so that you can be taxed. This is a simple process, which takes only a few days.

- Visit the New Kiwis website (see page 157), which specializes in placing migrants in appropriate jobs once they are based in New Zealand.
- If highly qualified, check out Hi-Q, New Zealand's specialist job-matching service (see page 157).
- Visit the websites run by local recruitment and temping agencies. (The New Zealand version of Google will help you to find them.)
- Look at job sections in the newspapers. The best appear on Monday, Wednesday and Saturday.
- Work and Income (New Zealand's social security agency) has free job-seeking services for unemployed residents (see 157).

If the going gets really tough, remember that you are not entitled to income support during your first two years in New Zealand. However, in circumstance of particular hardship you can apply to Work and Income (the social security agency, see page 157) for help.

Employment contracts

Employees' rights are covered by an Employment Agreement, which may be individual or collective. It covers things such as the minimum wage, holidays and parental leave, much of which is statutory, as well as any particular terms and conditions for the specific job.

An interesting aspect of New Zealand is that it is not a litigious society. This is because all accidents, including those at work, are covered by the government's Accident Insurance Scheme, run by the Accident Compensation Corporation. This handles all pay-outs, and an individual or company cannot be sued.

Many managers and professionals work more than a 40-hour week without being paid overtime. Workers on an hourly rate usually receive overtime pay for hours worked over those stated in their employment agreement. Overtime pay varies between industries.

The minimum wage for those aged over 18 is NZ$64 per eight-hour day in a 40-hour working week. Employees are entitled to 11 public holidays, plus three weeks' paid leave after working 12 months.

Get Healthy

The New Zealand Public Health Service is modern and relatively efficient. Waiting times vary according to area and the type of treatment, but that won't be anything new for Brits. Almost all hospital treatments and specialist consultations are free, but patients must pay for routine services, such as GP visits.

The Public Health Service covers:
- Free hospital treatment, including accident and emergency
- Free lab tests and x-rays
- Free health care during pregnancy and childbirth
- Free breast screening for women aged 50–65
- Subsidized GP fees
- Subsidized fees for osteopaths, physiotherapists and chiropractors
- Subsidized prescriptions

GPs

You can register free of charge with any GP and have the right to change at any time. Look under 'Registered Medical Practitioners and Medical Centres' in the phone book.

The full cost of seeing a GP is NZ$45–NZ$55 – more if you want a house call at night or the weekend. The government subsidizes children under six to the tune of NZ$35 per visit. Many doctors do not charge any fee on top, so treatment is free. The subsidy for those aged 6–17 is NZ$15.

Subsidies are also available to people on low incomes via the Community Services Card, and to those who have a condition requiring regular health care via the High Use Health Card. Contact your local Public Health Service office for details.

Private health care

Many New Zealanders opt for private health insurance schemes because private hospitals can offer immediate treatment of non-urgent conditions. Having private health insurance does not exclude you from the Public Health System and you still have to pay for it through direct taxation.

Hospitals

With a few minor exceptions, treatment at Public Health hospitals is free, although non-NZ residents may have to pay for some treatments.

In an emergency, go to the emergency unit of any public hospital. If you live in the back of beyond, find out where your nearest hospital is and plan your route there to save time when you need it.

Dental Care

School clinics give routine free dental check-ups to all schoolchildren. They can also give treatment, although many parents opt to go to a private dentist for this instead.

The Government Dental Benefit Scheme covers the cost of dental care from ages 13 to 18, but it is voluntary and not all dentists take part, so check before you register.

Charges for a standard check-up are NZ$50–NZ$90.

Pharmacies

Pharmacies, indicated by a green or red cross, are open during normal shopping hours. Those open until 10 or 11 p.m. are listed in the hospitals section of the phone book under 'Urgent Pharmacies'. When closed, details of the nearest 24-hour pharmacy will be posted on the door.

Prescriptions are free for children under six years old. Others pay between NZ$3 and NZ$15 per prescription for up to 20 prescriptions a year. After that they are free.

Get Wealthy

This section fills you in on handling your finances in New Zealand, covering everything from banks and bills to taxes and wills.

Banks

The banking system in New Zealand will be familiar to anyone coming from the UK. There are plenty of banks, including National Bank, TSB Bank, Bank of New Zealand, ANZ Bank and Kiwi Bank, and they're all highly competitive. The Consumer Institute has comparative information about the different banks (see page 157).

Most people use Internet or telephone banking to manage their money. The post office offer a separate online facility for bill paying (see page 157).

Opening a bank account

You can open a bank account in New Zealand even if you are not resident. If you are earning, you will need your IRD number (see page 144).

You will need...
- A permanent address (PO boxes and hotel addresses are not acceptable)
- Passport or driving licence

- A minimum deposit

Switch-type transactions, known as Electronic Fund Transfer at Point of Sale (EFTPOS), are the most popular method of payment. You must key in your PIN number when you pay.

The *Get a New Life* team relocated Paul and Julie Goddard and their children Zoe and Sam to New Zealand during the first series of the show. Paul is keen to advise people to budget carefully when they first arrive in New Zealand:

'The difference between wages here and in the UK is colossal. When you first come to New Zealand you convert everything to pounds and things seem ridiculously inexpensive. You look at cars and boats and think, "Blimey, that's cheap". You look at gorgeous houses that would cost a million pounds in the UK and you think you can suddenly afford them. But then you realize that, despite the lower wages, the cost of living in New Zealand is almost the same as that of the UK. The average wage where we are, in Tauranga in the North Island, is only about NZ$10 an hour (£3.50) and that's been very hard to adjust to. I'm self-employed and earn about four times that, but we're still struggling. Outside Auckland there aren't many major employers so very few people earn a really good wage.

Lots of people coming here from the UK blow it in the first few months. They splash all their cash on things that seem really cheap because they're still in English money mode, but then they get a nasty surprise and end up having to go home. There's a great lifestyle to be had here but you have to work really hard for it. If someone had told us we would be considerably worse off financially when we got here, we might have reconsidered.'

Cheques

Most retail outlets don't accept cheques because cheque guarantee cards aren't available in New Zealand. Most people pay by cash or with their EFTPOS card.

Withdrawing cash

The methods for withdrawing cash are the same as in the UK.

Bank charges

In general, you will notice that there are a lot more charges in New Zealand. You will be charged a basic service fee each month of about NZ$3–NZ$10, plus a variety of fees for services ranging from accepting cheques in shops to cash-machine withdrawals, manual transactions, electronic transfers … the list goes on. You may be able to avoid the charges if you maintain a minimum balance or have a mortgage with the bank.

Bank statements

As in the UK, most banks supply statements quarterly, unless you request them to be sent more frequently.

Banking hours

Banks are open Monday to Friday, 9 a.m. to 4.30 p.m. Of course, 24-hour cash machines are widely available.

Taxes

New Zealand is remarkably free of taxes. There is no capital gains tax or inheritance tax, no Stamp Duty and no road tax (unless you drive an HGV). In fact, there are likely to be only three taxes that will really affect you (see below).

The New Zealand tax year runs from 1 April to 31 March, and your employer should ensure you pay the right amount of tax. (You must give your IRD number to your employer when you start work.) You should also fill in a tax declaration code, otherwise you will be taxed at 45%. If you are receiving income from rent or a business, keep records and send your IR3 tax return to the Inland Revenue at the end of every tax year.

If you have paid too much or too little tax, or used the wrong tax code, you will be sent a personal tax summary in June. If you are entitled to a refund of less than NZ$200, it will be paid within 30 days of the summary being issued. Refunds over that amount will be paid once you confirm your personal tax summary.

If you have more tax to pay, it must be paid by 7 February, unless you have a tax agent or agreed extension, in which case the deadline is 7 April.

Some people must request a personal tax summary, but anyone can request one to ensure they have paid the correct amount of tax. Log on to the Inland Revenue website for more details (see page 157).

Income tax

This is paid on worldwide income, and is arranged in bands according to how much you earn. The top rate is 39% for income over NZ$60,001. It is usually paid straight from your wages via PAYE.

If you spend 183 days or more in New Zealand in any given year you are deemed to be a resident for tax purposes and will be taxed on your worldwide income. Non-tax residents will be taxed only on income made in New Zealand.

If you are thinking of setting up your own business or partnership, the top rate of business tax tends to be lower than the top rate of income tax, so even if you are a sole trader, it may be worth becoming a company. There is no limit on the amount of money you can take into New Zealand from abroad, although you do have to declare cash of more than NZ$10,000.

On moving to a new country you should always take advice from a professional when it comes to your finances. Situations change and conflicts may arise between New Zealand law and that in the UK.

Earner levy

Levied at source from wages, the earner levy goes towards the ACC accident compensation scheme and is paid at a rate of 1.2%.

General services tax (GST)

Similar to VAT, this is currently set at 12.5% on most transactions.

Social Security

It is unlikely you will be able to claim any benefits during your first two years in New Zealand, but you could do some research into your particular situation by logging on to the government's Work and Income website (see page 157). The Citizens Advice Bureau, which has many branches in New Zealand, can also advise you of your rights.

Pensions

In line with people in many other countries, most New Zealanders take out their own private pension scheme to supplement their state pension. Employer pensions schemes are rare in New Zealand.

Wills

Whenever and wherever you are writing a will, it always makes sense to consult a professional. Laws vary, so you have to make sure your New Zealand will does not clash with any UK will you may have.

Unlike the UK, where you can leave whatever you want to whoever you like, New Zealand has rules that give certain rights to your partner (married, de facto or same sex) and any children or stepchildren of a relationship. If you die intestate, or your will does not fulfil these rights, the estate can be challenged under certain laws, including the Property (Relationships) Act 1976.

Get Wise

Education is free up to the age of eighteen, but compulsory only from six to sixteen. However, children are allowed to start soon after their fifth birthday, and most do. Class sizes vary according to area. Urban schools can have up to 30 pupils in a class, while those in rural areas may have small classes, with different age groups being taught together.

Parents have to pay for any uniform required, as well as stationery. Most schools also have an annual voluntary donation to help with running costs, which most parents pay.

Provided you are a New Zealand citizen or have a Resident's Permit or Work Permit, your children are considered resident and are entitled to free education. If you don't have the necessary NZIS permit, you will be charged.

Choosing a school can be tough when you are trying to find your feet in a new country, but help is at hand. The Education Review Office (ERO) is responsible for reporting on standards in primary and secondary schools. Their reports, as well as booklets on how to choose schools for different ages, are available from the ERO website (see page 157). League tables for academic results at secondary schools are published by the New Zealand Qualifications Authority (see page 157).

Private schools are subject to the same ERO reports as state schools. The fees vary widely and the better ones could well have one- or two-year waiting lists for admission.

Once you have identified a good school and are dead set on your child going there, the only way to make sure of a place is to buy a house within its catchment area. There may be a limited number of places open to those from outside the area, but these are often awarded through lotteries.

When enrolling a child, most difficulty is caused by the fact that the New Zealand school year runs from January to December, while the British one runs from September to July. Your child will therefore have to skip or repeat six months of schooling. It is best to contact your chosen school as soon as possible and they will advise you as to which year your child should join. Note that some schools may have waiting lists.

New Zealand's education system

Here's a quick rundown of what you can expect to encounter when you dip a toe into New Zealand's education system.

Pre-school, ages 1 to 5–6

This includes kindergartens, education and care centres, playgroups and home-based childcare. Much of it is not government funded and must be paid for. The government agency called Early Child Development (ECD, see page 157) provides local contacts and advice on what is available in your area.

Primary school, ages 5–6 to 11–12

Most children start primary education at age five. Many schools have the equivalent of a reception class in the first year of school, and formal education starts in the second year.

Secondary school, ages 12–13 to 16, 17 or 18

Known variously as high school, college or grammar school. Pupils work towards National Certificates of Educational Achievement (NCEAs) – public exams equivalent to GCSEs, A/S and A levels. Coursework accounts for 40% of the results.

Level 1 is taken in the fifth form (age 16) and is equivalent to GCSE.
Level 2 is taken in the sixth form (age 17) and is equivalent to A/S level.
Level 3 is taken in the seventh form (age 18) and is equivalent to A level.

School year

The academic year runs from late January to early or mid-December and is split into four terms: late January to mid-April; late April to late June; mid-July to mid-September; early October to mid-December. There are breaks of about two weeks between the terms, with a 6–8-week break for the summer. There are no half-terms, but schools close on public holidays.

School hours are 9 a.m. to 3 p.m. for primary schools and 9 a.m. to 3.30 p.m. for secondary schools. There is generally a one-hour break for lunch, as well as short morning and afternoon breaks.

Get Around

The thing that will most strike you when travelling around New Zealand is the s-p-a-c-e. Roads are uncongested and traffic jams are rare. And on public transport you don't get standing room only, with your face jammed in someone else's armpit – that unlovely characteristic found on so much of Britain's public transport.

On the road

Driving in New Zealand is generally an enjoyable experience. The roads are well maintained, congestion is rare and they drive on the left, so Brits won't have any trouble adjusting.

Your UK driving licence is valid in New Zealand for up to 12 months. At some point during that time you will have to apply for a New Zealand licence, pass an eye test and a written and practical driving test. Make sure you do this in good time. If the 12 months are up before you've got your New Zealand licence, you will be considered to be driving without a licence.

Driving Tips

- It is compulsory to carry your driving licence at all times.
- The speed limit is 50 km/h in built-up areas, 100 km/h on highways and 50 or 70 km/h in Limited Speed Zones (LSZ), such as outside schools and retirement homes, and approaching pedestrian and rail crossings.
- Seat-belts must be worn at all times in the back and front seats.
- The driver is responsible for making sure all children under five are in a suitable car seat.
- Drink-driving leads to an immediate loss of licence and a fine or imprisonment.
- Rural roads may be unsurfaced, so make sure your vehicle can cope with them.
- Cyclists and motorcyclists must wear helmets.
- Always park with the flow of the traffic. Parking facing against the flow is illegal.

Insurance

Prepare to be gobsmacked: insurance is not compulsory in New Zealand – unbelievable but true.

Although many New Zealanders don't bother to get it, we think it's advisable to have at least third-party insurance to avoid a hefty bill if you do smash up someone else's car.

More information about driving in New Zealand is available from the Land Transport Safety Authority (see page 157).

Trains

Tranz Scenic is the main passenger-carrying service in New Zealand, and provides excellent coverage on the main trunk lines. Certain small rural routes are disappearing, and the government is having to step in to keep some services running. The good news is that commuter services in Auckland and Wellington are relatively efficient, and the trains across the country are clean, modern and air-conditioned.

Buses

Local and intercity buses are ubiquitous and cheap. Advance-purchase fares are available on intercity services and can save you up to 30%.

Internal flights

It is easy to get around New Zealand by plane, but relatively expensive. Most services are operated by Air New Zealand or Qantas, with small scheduled and charter operators running localized services.

Get a Life

The weather in New Zealand may not be quite so reliably gorgeous as in Australia, but Kiwis are as sports mad as their Australian cousins. Life revolves around rugby, swimming, bungee-jumping, canoeing ... you name it.

Paul Goddard and his family love the outdoor life they are able to lead in New Zealand, and as Paul says:

'New Zealand is fantastic for kids. There's so much for them to do. We live by the beach and they can go surfing every day if they want to. Kids are allowed to be kids here.'

The wide open spaces of New Zealand make walking one of life's greatest pleasures. Everyone does it, yet you can walk for miles and never see anyone else. Fantastic! Remember, though, that the sun really is stronger in the southern hemisphere, and you can burn within ten minutes, so *always* wear a sunscreen.

Making friends

New Zealanders are relaxed, friendly, unpretentious and open, so it is more than likely that within days of moving into your new home a gaggle of neighbours will have been round to say hello, pass the time of day and generally check you out.

New Zealand is definitely its own unique country, and ties with Britain, particularly among the young, are far looser than they were. But at times New Zealand can seem so much like home that it's easy to forget you are in someone else's country. Cultural differences are more difficult to spot and gaffes are easier to make, so take care not to offend.

Expats

The British expat community isn't quite such a sore thumb in New Zealand as it can be in other countries. We tend to settle in well, helped by a common language, heritage and, yes, the dear old Queen popping up from time to time.

If you are yearning for the sound of Estuary English, someone to reminisce with or to moan about New Zealand's lack of traffic, crime or pollution, you won't have to look far. Most of the population is descended from Brits and we just keep on coming. The British Consulate is a good place to start for lists of expat clubs and societies.

Shopping

You may at first wonder why everyone keeps talking about 'dairies'. These are the equivalent of our local corner shops, and are just as useful for the day-to-day basics and finding out what's going on in the community.

For decades New Zealand shoppers suffered from restrictive trade laws, which prevented foreign goods being imported, or slapped high import taxes on those that got through. Today you can get just about anything, and at reasonable prices, too. The country benefits from cheap cars and electrical goods thanks to its relative proximity to Asia.

Although haggling is not part of life in New Zealand, if you are spending a lot – and you may well be if you are furnishing your home from scratch – it is worth asking if there is any discount available. The worst they can do is say no, and a yes could save you a tidy sum.

Opening hours

Most shops are open Monday to Friday, 9 a.m. to 5 p.m, with a couple of late nights and shorter hours at the weekend. However, there are numerous large shopping centres that open seven days a week from 9 a.m. to 10 p.m. Additionally, many supermarkets are open 24 hours a day, seven days a week.

Going out

The outdoors is New Zealand's finest asset, and most of its economy is tied up with the countryside. The natural bounty that gives rise to everything from forestry to wine making, and farming to tourism, is also closely bound up with leisure, and most people like nothing better than to socialize outside.

Even in the major cities of Auckland and Wellington, few people are more than 20 minutes from the beach. Go inland and you will find mountains with wonderful skiing, walks to die for and rivers with 'trout the size of

salmon'. In fact, fishing is a national obsession, and consequently boat ownership is high. And don't forget, the extreme sport of bungee-jumping started here.

New Zealand's small population, good transport and attitude that says there's more to life than work mean that its natural assets are enjoyed all the time – not just on rare weekends, but on ordinary evenings after work. However, New Zealand's towns and cities are rapidly giving the great outdoors a bit of competition. They have leapt forward in recent years and are no longer sleepy, post-colonial backwaters, but culturally vibrant, with plenty to offer every taste. This is particularly evident in the food. 'Slam in the Lamb' went out of fashion long ago, and today New Zealand cuisine is innovative, exciting and exceptionally good value for money.

New Zealanders rarely tip, unless service really is outstanding. Many Kiwi waiters and bar staff look out for foreign tourists, as they know they're more likely to get a tip from them than from a native New Zealander.

Tips For Social Success

- Kiwis are proud of their classless society, so airs, graces and general lording it do not go down well.
- New Zealanders don't tend to kiss when they meet. A handshake and hello do the trick.
- As in the UK, it's polite to address someone older than you by their title (Mr, Mrs or Dr So-and-so) until you are invited to call them by their first name.
- Rugby is a national obsession, so think twice before you break into 'Swing Low Sweet Chariot'.
- Similarly with cricket, it's best to be discreet – not that the recent form of the England team is likely to give you much to crow about.

Staying in touch

The New Zealand postal service is very efficient, despite the fact that postcodes are rarely used. Airmail takes 2–3 days to reach Europe.

The New Zealand telephone system (Telecom New Zealand) is modern and efficient.

To telephone New Zealand from the UK dial 00 64 and omit the first zero of the New Zealand number.
To telephone the UK from New Zealand dial 00 44 and omit the first zero of the UK number.

International telephone rates from New Zealand are very inexpensive. The best time to call home is in the evenings (6.00 p.m. to 6.00 a.m.) and at weekends (6.00 p.m. Friday to 6.00 a.m. Monday), you can make two hours of calls to the UK for NZ$8.00.

Emergencies

In an emergency dial 111 for the police, fire brigade or ambulance service.

In general, New Zealand is a safe environment. Kids walk to school on their own, in rural areas doors are left unlocked, and the egalitarian nature of the Kiwis makes for a low crime rate. Of course crime exists, and is often drug related, but that's no surprise. The main problem is car crime, so don't leave valuables on show, and make sure you lock the car.

Useful Addresses

European Union

Academic Qualifications Recognition

The National Academic Recognition Information Centre for the United Kingdon (UK Naric)
Ecctis Ltd
Oriel House
Oriel Road
Cheltenham
Gloucestershire
GL50 1XP
Tel: 0870 9904088
www.naric.org.uk

Foreign Office Legalisation Service
The Legalisation Office
Foreign and Commonwealth Office
Old Admiralty Building
The Mall
London SW1A 2LG
Open Monday to Friday, 10 a.m.–12 p.m. and 2 p.m.–3 p.m.
Tel: 020 7008 1111
www.fco.gov.uk/legalisation

Benefits

Foreign & Commonwealth Office
www.fco.gov.uk

European Commission (UK)
8 Storey's Gate
London SW1P 3AT
Tel: 020 7973 1992
Fax: 020 7973 1900
www.europe.org.uk

Windsor House
9–15 Bedford Street
Belfast BT2 7EG
Tel: 028 9024 0708
Fax: 028 9024 8241
www.cec.org.uk/ni/index.htm

2 Caspian Point
Caspian Way
Cardiff CF10 4QQ
Tel: 029 2089 5020
Fax: 029 2089 5035
www.cec.org.uk/wales/index.htm

9 Alva Street
Edinburgh EH2 4PH
Tel: 0131 225 2058
Fax: 0131 226 4105
www.cec.org.uk/scotland/index.htm

Europe Direct
Part of the European Commission
Freephone 00800 6789 1011
http://europa.eu.int has a wealth of information about getting work permits in all EU countries, plus guides and factsheets specific to your chosen destination.
http://europa.eu.int/eures for lists of jobs in all EU countries, and for EU housing, living and working information.

European Ombudsman
1 Avenue du Prés. R. Schuman
BP 403
F-67001 Strasbourg Cedex
France
Tel: +33 3 88 17 23 13
Fax: +33 3 88 17 90 62
www.euro-ombudsman.eu.int

European Parliament
European Parliament Information Office
2 Queen Anne's Gate
London SW1H 9AA
Tel: 020 7227 4300
Fax: 020 7227 4302
www.europarl.eu.int

Motoring

DVLA
Long View Road
Swansea SA6 7JL
Tel: 0870 2400 009
Fax: 01792 783071
www.dvla.gov.uk

Pensions

Department for Work and Pensions (DWP)
International Pension Centre
Tyneview Park
Newcastle-upon-Tyne
NE98 1BA
Tel: 0191 218 7777
Fax: 0191 218 7293
www.thepensionservice.gov.uk

Relocation Specialists

Association of Relocation Agents
PO Box 189
Diss
Norfolk IP22 1PE
Tel: 08700 737475
Fax: 08700 718719
www.relocationagents.com

Rights in EU

EFTA Secretariat
74 rue de Trèves
B-1040 Brussels
Belgium
Tel: +32 2 286 1711
Fax: +32 2 286 1750
http://secretariat.efta.int

Skill Recognition

Department for Education and Skills
Room E3B
Moorfoot
Sheffield S1 4PQ
Tel: 0114 2594151
Fax: 0114 2594475
www.dfes.gov.uk/europeopen
Operates UK Certificates of Experience scheme.

Work

www.jobcentreplus.gov.uk
http://europa.eu.int/eures

International Herald Tribune (London office)
www.iht.com

France

British Representation in France

British Embassy
35 rue Faubourg St Honoré
75383 Paris
Cedex 08
Tel: +33 1 44 51 31 00
Fax: +33 1 44 51 41 27
www.amb-grandbretagne.fr

Franco-British Chamber of Commerce and Industry
31 rue Boissy d'Anglas
75008 Paris
Tel: +33 1 53 30 81 30
Fax: +33 1 53 30 81 35
www.francobritishchamber.com

Buying Property

www.avendrealouer.fr
www.hestia.fr

Buildings insurance
www.axa.fr
www.agf.fr

Education

British Council
www.britishcouncil.org/france/france-education

Ministère de L'Education Nationale
Ministère de la jeunesse, de l'éducation nationale
et de la recherche
110 rue de Grenelle
75357 Paris
cedex 07
Tel: +33 1 55 55 10 10
www.education.gouv.fr
For information about state schools.

**Centre d'Information et de Documentation
de l'Enseignement Privé**
6 rue Monsigny
75002 Paris
Tel: +33 1 44 55 34 80
www.enseignement-prive.info
For information about independent schools.

French Customs Service

Direction des Douanes
www.douane.gouv.fr

French Health Service

www.cpam-paris.fr

French Representation in Britain

French Embassy
58 Knightsbridge
London SW1X 7JT
UK
Tel: 020 7073 1000
www.ambafrance-uk.org

Travel

French Railways
SNCF
Tel: +33 8 36 57 68 69
www.sncf.fr
www.tgv.fr

Work

Recruitment Specialists
www.apr-job.com
www.adecco.fr
www.manpower.fr
www.job.fr

**Ministre d'Emploi et Solidarité
(Ministry for Social Affairs, Labour
and Solidarity)**
www.travail.gouv.fr
For information about working conditions.

Newspapers
www.lemonde.fr
www.lefigaro.fr
www.lexpress.fr

Spain

British Community in Spain

British Embassy
Calle Fernando el Santo, 16
28010 Madrid
Tel: +34 91 700 8200 or 91 319 0200
Fax: +34 91 700 8272

British Consulate-General
Paseo de Recoletos 7/9
28004 Madrid
Tel: +34 91 524 97 00
Fax: +34 91 524 97 30
www.ukinspain.com
For British Consulate listings throughout Spain.

Business/Investment

**Instituto Español de Comercio Exterior
(ICEX)**
Departamento de Asesoría Jurídica y
Administración
Paseo de la Castellana 14–16
28046 Madrid
Tel: +34 91 349 6100
Fax: +34 91 349 6128
http://portal.icex.es

Invest in Spain
Office for Economic and Commercial Affairs
Embassy of Spain
66 Chiltern Street
London W1U 4LS
UK
Tel: 020 7467 2330
Fax: 020 7487 5586
www.mcx.es/londres/
www.investinspain.org

Ministerio de Economía
Dirección General de Comercio e Inversiones
(General Directorate for Trade and Investment)
Paseo de la Castellana 162, Planta 7
28046 Madrid
Tel: +34 91 349 3983
Fax: +34 91 349 3562
www.mcx.es/polco/default.htm

Buying Property

**Foundation Institute of Foreign Property
Owners**
Apartado 418
Calle la Mar 193
03590 Altea
Alicante
Tel: +34 96 584 2312
Fax: +34 96 584 1589
www.fipe.org

Education

British Council
http://www.britishcouncil.es

Spanish Ministry of Education
Ministerio de educación, cultura y deporte
Calle Alcalá, 36
28071 Madrid
Tel: +34 91 701 8000 or
90 221 8500 (9.00 a.m.–4.30 p.m.)
Fax: +34 91 701 8648
www.mec.es

Relocation Services

www.relocatetospain.com
www.spanishrelocation.com
www.reloc8.net
www.idealspain.com
www.relocatedelsol.com (specialises in the
Costa del Sol)

Residence Permits

Ministerio del Interior
Delegacion del Gobierno para la Extranjeria y la
Inmigracion
Amador de los Rios, 5-7
28071 Madrid
Tel: +34 91 537 1000
Fax: +34 91 578 1087
www.mir.es

Social Security

Instituto Nacional de la Seguridad Social
Subdirección General de Relaciones
Internacionales
Padre Damian 4
28036 Madrid
Tel: +34 91 564 7681
www.seg-social.es

Spanish Representation in the UK

Spanish Embassy
39 Chesham Place
London SW1X 8SB
UK
Tel: 020 7235 5555
Fax: 020 7259 5392
www.mcx.es/londres/

Tax Office of the Spanish Government

www.aeat.es (Spanish only)

Travel

Spanish Airlines
Iberia: www.iberia.com
Air Europa: www.air-europa.com

Spanish Railways
RENFE
Tel: +34 90 224 0202
www.renfe.es

Work

Spanish Labour Office in UK
Tel: 020 7221 0098
Fax: 020 7229 7270

Italy

British Representation in Italy

British Embassy in Rome
Via XX Settembre 80
1-00187 Roma RM
Tel: +39 06 4220 0001
Fax: +39 06 4220 2334
www.britain.it

Buying Property

http://realestate.escapeartist.com
www.europropertydirect.co.uk
www.italy-real-estate.net
www.rural-retreats-italy.com

Codice Fiscale

www.finanze.it

Expat Community

www.luccagrapevine.com
www.informer.it
www.hellomilano.it
www.wantedinrome.com

English Yellow Pages
Via Belisario 4/b
00187 Rome
Tel: +39 06 4740 861
Website: www.englishyellowpages.it
Listings for English-speaking professionals and
organizations in many of the major cities and
surrounding areas.

Italian Representation in Britain

Embassy of Italy
14 Three Kings Yard
London W1K 4EH
UK
Tel: 020 7312 2200
Fax: 020 7499 2283
www.embitaly.org.uk

Italian Consulate General
38 Eaton Place
London SW1X 8AN
UK
Tel: 020 7235 9371
Fax: 020 7823 1609
www.embitaly.org.uk

Motoring

Automobile Club d'Italia (ACI)
www.aci.it

Taxation

Agenzia delle Entrate (tax office)
www.agenziaentrate.it

Australia

Australian Representation in Britain

Australian Honorary Consuls
69 George Street
Edinburgh EH2 2JG
UK
Tel: 0131 624 3333
Fax: 0131 624 3701

1st Floor
Century House
11 St Peter's Square
Manchester M2 3DN
UK
Tel: 0161 237 9440
Fax: 0161 237 9135

Australian High Commission
Strand
London WC2B 4LA
UK
Tel: 020 7379 4334
Fax: 020 7240 5333
www.australia.org.uk
Migration branch open: Monday to Friday,
9 a.m. to 11 a.m., except for British and
Australian public holidays.

Building Your Own Home

Royal Australian Institute of Architects
PO Box 3373
MANUKA ACT 2603
Tel: +61 2 6273 1548
Fax: +61 2 6273 1953
www.architecture.com.au

Business/Investment

Foreign Investment Review Board
www.firb.gov.au

Buying Property

www.realestate.com.au
www.property-abroad.com/ausnz.asp
See also newspaper websites.

First Home Owner Grant
www.firsthome.gov.au

Car Registration

www.samarins.com

Citizenship

www.immi.gov.au/e_visa/citizen.htm

Education

**Commonwealth Department of Education,
Training and Youth Affairs**
www.detya.gov.au
For information about choosing schools.

Private schools
www.privateschoolsaustralia.com.au

Health

Australian government site
http://www.health.gov.au
http://www.hic.gov.au

Cancer Council Australia
www.cancer.org.au

Immigration Assistance

**Migration Agents' Registration Authority
(MARA)**
PO Box Q1551
QVB NSW 1230
Tel: +61 2 9299 5446
Fax: +61 2 9299 8448
www.themara.com.au

Pet Importation Forms
Department of Agriculture, Fisheries and
Forestry (AFF)
www.affa.gov.au

Renting Property

www.gomatilda.com/realestate
www.homesonline.com.au

VISAS

**Department of Immigration and Multicultural
and Indigenous Affairs (DIMIA)**
Migration Branch
Australian High Commission
Strand
London WC2B 4LA
UK
Tel: 020 7379 4334
Fax: 020 7465 8218
www.australia.org.uk
www.immi.gov.au
Visa information is also available from:
www.migrationexpert.com
www.australiamigrate.co.uk

**Business Skills (Provisional) Visas
and Business Talent Visas**
Perth Business Skills Processing Centre (PBSPC)
Locked Bag Number 7
Northbridge WA 6865
Tel: +61 8 9415 9215
Fax: +61 8 9415 9291
Website:
www.immi.gov.au/business/bcperthoffshore.htm

Skilled Australian Sponsored Visa
General Skilled Migration
Adelaide Skilled Processing Centre
GPO Box 1638
Adelaide
South Australia 5001
Tel: +61 3 9657 4115
Fax: +61 8 8237 6629
Email: adelaide.skilled.centre@immi.gov.au

Travel

Rail Australia
www.railaustralia.com.au

Wills
www.law4u.com.au

Work

Australian government site
www.workplace.gov.au

Newspapers
http://www.nla.gov.au/npapers

New Zealand

British Representation in New Zealand

British High Commission
44 Hill Street
PO 1812
Thorndon
Wellington
Tel: +64 4 924 2888
Fax: +64 4 473 4982
www.britain.org.nz

Citzenship

Department of Internal Affairs (DIA)
46 Waring Taylor Street
PO Box 805
Wellington
Tel: +64 4 474 8123
www.dia.govt.nz

Education

Education Review Office (ERO)
Level 1, 101 Lambton Quay
Box 2799
Wellington
Tel: +64 4 499 2489
Fax: +64 4 499 2482
www.ero.govt.nz

Early Child Development
Early Childhood Information Centre
Ministry of Education
45-47 Pipitea Street
PO Box 666
Thorndon
Wellington
Tel: +64 4 463 8000
Fax: +64 4 463 8001
www.ecdu.govt.nz

Immigration Assistance

Move to New Zealand
www.movetonz.govt.nz
A helpful government site with general information about living in New Zealand.

New Zealand Immigration Service (NZIS)
New Zealand House
80 Haymarket
London SW1Y 4TQ
UK
Tel: 09069 100 100 (£1 per minute)
Fax: 0207 973 0370
www.immigration.govt.nz

New Zealand Association for Migration and Investment (NZAMI)
For a list of immigration consultants
Website: www.nzami.co.nz

Student visa
You can download a form (using Adobe Acrobat) from www.immigration.govt.nz/study
Forms can also be ordered over the phone: 09069 100 100. Calls cost £1 per minute.

On Arrival New Zealand
Tel: +64 4 237 7710
Fax: +64 4 237 9812
www.onarrival.co.nz
This company aims to provide a complete 'end to end' service for families moving to New Zealand.

Pet Importation Permit
Import Management
Ministry of Agriculture and Forestry
PO Box 2526
Wellington
Tel: +64 4 498 9625
Fax: +64 4 474 4132
www.maf.govt.nz

Money

Online bill-paying
www.ebill.co.nz

Bank comparisons
Consumer Institute
www.consumer.org.nz

Motoring

Land Transport Safety Authority
www.ltsa.govt.nz

Newspapers

New Zealand Outlook
Tel: 01424 223111
www.consylpublishing.co.uk

Destination New Zealand
Tel: 01323 726040
www.destination-newzealand.com

New Zealand Customs Service

The Customhouse
17-21 Whitmore Street
Box 2218
Wellington
Tel: +64 4 473 6099
Fax: +64 4 473 7370
www.customs.govt.nz

New Zealand Representation in Britain

New Zealand High Commission
New Zealand House
80 Haymarket
London SW1Y 4TE
Tel: 020 7930 8422
Fax: 020 7839 4580
www.nzembassy.com/uk

Property

Newspapers
www.nzherald.co.nz/property
www.propertystuff.co.nz

Private sales
www.propertyweb.co.nz

Real Estate Institute of New Zealand
www.realenz.co.uk
Lists of property for sale all over the country.

Short-Term Accomodation
www.yellowpages.co.nz

Tenancy Services
www.tenancy.govt.nz

Social Security
Work and Income
PO Box 12136
Wellington
Tel: +64 9 913 0300
www.winz.govt.nz

Taxation

Inland Revenue Department
National Office
PO Box 2198
Wellington
Tel: +64 4 801 9973
www.ird.govt.nz

Work

Checking qualifications
www.movetonz.govt.nz
www.nzqa.govt.nz

Job listings
www.nzherald.co.nz
www.careers.co.nz
www.alljobs.co.nz

Job-placement agency for migrants
www.newkiwis.co.nz

Setting Up Your Own Business
www.investnewzealand.govt.nz

Specialist job-matching service for the highly qualified
www.hi-q.org.nz

Specialist teaching sites
www.edgazette.govt.nz
www.teachnz.govt.nz

Index

Acknowledgements

This book would not be possible without the dedication and determination of the outstandingly talented Brighter Pictures production and creative teams. Without their endless enthusiasm and belief in the projects, neither the series or the book would have been possible.

We'd both like to thank everyone at BBC Books, especially Nicky Ross and Sarah Emsley for their great enthusiasm and guidance throughout this project.

A big thanks also to the relocators who've put their lives on hold – Melissa Porter and Scott Huggins, and Jonathan Jay and Tina Korup – and to their partners who've supported them during the long months away.

Many, many thanks to Susannah Walker, Susan Crook, Philippa Farnese, Oliver Tait, Helen Nightingale and their teams who made it happen. You've all been amazingly dedicated and focused.

A big thank-you to the Brighter Pictures development team: Richard Brooks, Jonathan Stadlen and Ricky Cooper who've worked on the series from the very first draft of the proposal and still bring their energy and inspiration to the series, and James Brett-Young for the additional research. To Luke Wilkins, thank-you for taking care of business.

Jane Root, Nicola Moody, Jo Clinton-Davies, Richard Klein and Tom Archer at the BBC who have supported the programme from the germ of an idea through to the success that it is today. Thank-you.

We would also like to thank the following for helping to guide us through the maze of bureaucracy that relocating your life often entails: Tad Zurlinden and Dominic Tidey at the European Relocation Association; Tom Hoskin at the Foreign Office; Ian Johnson at Global Visas, London; Julie Graney at Nevett Ford Lawyers, Melbourne, Australia; Margaret Mccartney at Expat International, Melbourne, Australia; Laura Sobrero at the Italian Embassy, London; Catherine McMaster, psychotherapist.

Finally, an enormous and heartfelt thank you to all the families who've moved, or are in the process of moving, for their courage determination and patience. You're all a great source of inspiration to thousands of other families who share your dreams.

Remy Blumenfeld and Gavin Hay

Anna Elsey would like to give huge thanks to Jim and Wendy Elsey and Mark, Jane and Phil Howarth for being world champion babysitters. And thanks to Ged and Florrie for being so good.

Anna Coombes would like to thank Seona and Les for time off work to do this, Richard for convincing me that I could, the other Anna for sharing the responsibility and mostly Bridgit, Ashley and Martha for their unfailing support.

BBC Worldwide would like to thank the following for providing photographs and permission to reproduce copyright material. While every effort has been made to trace and acknowledge all copyright holders, we would like to apologise should there have been any errors or omissions.

Alamy 153; Australian Picture Library 108, 118; Axiom 27; Corbis 6, 18, 20, 22, 32, 40, 46, 48, 58, 61, 73, 84, 114, 125, 130, 142, 144; Empics 86; Getty Images 16, 35, 53, 64, 88, 95; Iconica 25; ImageState 44; Lonely Planet Images © Richard l'Anson 17; Pictures Colour Library 100; Robert Harding 78; Robin Matthews 4; Travel Ink 13.